re Walmsley is a well-known television producer who
made a wide range of programmes on social, political
financial issues, including *Forty Minutes*, *Everyman*,
ight and *The Money Programme*. In 1990 she left the
and set up her own company, Boxclever, which
ses in presentation skills.

nally, she trained as a music teacher at the Royal Col-
Music in London. Her interest in assertiveness devel-
s a result of a variety of jobs and her experiences as a
nd mother.

the 1970s Claire Walmsley started running training
es in the northwest of England, for women returning to
, and redundant executives. She continued her interest
sertiveness whilst working for the BBC, and now teaches
onal development and presentation skills to companies
individuals.

laire Walmsley is married, has three children, two cats
d a granddaughter.

ASSERTIVENESS
□ THE RIGHT TO BE YOU □

Claire Walmsley

Cartoons by Sophie Grillet

BBC BOOKS

This book is dedicated to my family who first taught me about assertiveness. Their love and support throughout the writing of the book has kept me going.

My special thanks go to Frances and Jennie for encouragement, criticism and proof-reading.

To Alexis for being understanding.

To Mustapha for his wonderful help on the word-processor.

To Stephen for his positive encouragement and support.

To Iman for arriving in the middle of it all.

Published by BBC Books
a division of BBC Enterprises Limited,
Woodlands, 80 Wood Lane, London W12 0TT
First published 1991
© Claire Walmsley 1991

Reprinted 1992, 1993, 1994 (twice)

ISBN 0 563 36308 8

Set in Times New Roman by Ace Filmsetting Ltd, Frome, Somerset
Printed in England by Clays Ltd, St Ives plc
Cover printed by Clays Ltd, St Ives plc

Contents

Introduction

Assertiveness is about the way we behave in our relationships with other people. It's about developing relationships based on honesty and openness, where saying what you feel about things and what you want to happen is a normal experience.

Many people find that they are able to behave assertively in one relationship but not in another. For example, someone who is confident and assertive in relationships at work may find it very difficult to say 'No' to relatives at home. Others may find that they are capable of saying what they feel to their family, but are unable to act assertively with a manager of a shop or restaurant.

When I was asked to write the book to accompany and go beyond the television series, I decided to look at the way assertiveness can improve all these relationships. By understanding more about our behaviour in different situations, we can begin to see how we relate to other people, what they think about us, and what the advantages of behaving assertively might be.

Each of the four chapters concentrates on a different aspect of your lives where assertiveness can help;

Your relationship with yourself
Your relationship with your family and friends
Your relationship at work
Your relationship with people in your community.

Assertiveness has never been more necessary than it is now in the 1990s. Some of the changes in our society mean that we frequently face unpleasant experiences. Not only do we have to learn to deal with manipulative families, rude shop assistants or friends who make unreasonable demands on us, but we often have to sort out unhelpful bureaucracies, help our children to survive bullying, and deal with sexual harassment or racial abuse. All of these, sometimes distressing experiences, are ones where assertiveness can help. By learning to be assertive in our relationships we begin to take more control of our lives.

This is a 'How to' book, with practical suggestions and ideas which will help you to tackle difficult everyday situations and learn how to let people know what you want. It's written for men and women who are already trying to be assertive, as well as those who are quite new to the idea.

It doesn't require you to go on a course or read lots of other books. It is written as a friendly guide with practical exercises which will give you a taste of assertiveness, and let you decide for yourself if you like what you experience.

The chapters all follow the same pattern. At the beginning there is a list of Objectives which tell you what you can hope to achieve from working through the chapter, from making mundane everyday decisions to grabbing life by the scruff of the neck and becoming a 'new you'.

Then follows a Summary which makes it easy for you to see what's included, and why you might want to read that particular chapter.

Every chapter includes several Exercises which help you to find out more about yourself and the way you behave in different situations.

At the end of each chapter there is your own Personal Action Plan to help you to plan your own way forward.

On pages 10–11 is a questionnaire which will help you to see how you behave at the moment – whether you are aggressive, passive or assertive.

Where to start

Remember, your assertive muscles need to get into training, so don't start with the most challenging thing in your life – leave that for next week. Try practising on some situations where you know you have a chance of changing things. It's a bit like training for the Marathon, you need to start off with gentle exercise first. But wherever you start, remember that being assertive in one area will also help you to be more assertive in others. Once you get the hang of it, you will gain confidence to tackle some of the more difficult things in your life.

Enjoy it!

Questionnaire:
How Assertive are You?

Find out how assertive you are by deciding how you would react in the different circumstances described here.

(1) Your parents ask you to visit them. You find out that their friends, Joan and Bob, people you dislike, will be there. You don't want to go. Do you:

a. Agree to go. That's what's expected of you.
b. Say you know they would be upset if you didn't go, but tell them you're fed up about having to see their friends again.
c. Flatly refuse the invitation.
d. Say how you feel: although you would like to see them you don't want to see Joan and Bob. Perhaps arrange another day?

(2) Your partner comes home upset about something. Do you say:

a. 'It's all right for you. I've had a hell of a day, too.'
b. 'I can see you're upset. Would you like to talk about it?'
c. 'What's the matter with you again?'
d. Don't react. Ignore him or her all evening?

(3) You feel very angry about something. Do you:

a. Tell people directly that you are angry and why.
b. Sulk or go into a corner and seethe.
c. Let everyone know by being noisy or huffing and puffing.
d. React physically with rage?

(4) A colleague at work smokes heavily. You hate smoking because it gives you a headache. Do you:

a. Leave articles on smoking and cancer lying on the desk.
b. Keep opening windows and hiding ashtrays.
c. Tell him or her she's a selfish, inconsiderate person.
d. Tell him or her that you are allergic to smoke. Ask if it's possible to limit smoking in your office. Suggest that the tea-bar is where most smokers congregate?

(5) You buy a new suit. Your daughter says it's awful. Do you:

a. Feel dreadful and take it off.
b. Wait for an opportunity to get your own back on her.
c. Ask for more specific information. Check it out with someone else and make your own mind up.
d. Tell her you don't care a damn what she thinks and anyway she has no dress sense?

(6) A friend is constantly late for meetings. She always apologises, but it happens every time. Do you say:

a. 'I think it's unfair of you always to keep me waiting. I would feel happier if you could turn up on time in future.'
b. 'No, I didn't mind waiting.'
c. 'It's nice of you to turn up!'
d. 'Where the hell have you been again?'

(7) You have lent someone money. You want it repaying and he or she seems to have forgotten. What do you do?

a. Make veiled comments about how hard up you are.
b. Hope he or she will remember it eventually.
c. Take him or her one side. Say you were happy to lend money on condition that it was repaid. You now need it back.
d. Confront him or her in public and say you've waited long enough to be paid back?

(8) You have stayed at home all day for your usually reliable electrician. He doesn't turn up. What do you do?

a. Feel mad but decide to wait and see what happens.
b. Phone and ask what he thinks he's doing.
c. Phone. Shout about unreliability and slam the phone down.
d. Phone. Ask him to explain why they didn't arrive. Arrange another appointment, adding that you took time off work. If he fails to turn up again, you will send a bill?

Turn to page 141 for the scores.

CHAPTER ONE

Assertiveness and You

OBJECTIVES

To help you to:
- find out more about assertiveness
- find out how assertive you are
- understand behaviour
- identify your needs, feelings and rights
- understand other people's rights and feelings
- build your confidence and self esteem
- communicate better
- deal with everyday situations

SUMMARY

What exactly is assertiveness?
Why be assertive?
Behaviour: fight, flight or communication
Your rights
Using your head: knowing what you want
Communication: finding the right words
Communication: body language
Involving a partner: role play
Feedback
Putting it into practice
Techniques for dealing with other people's reactions
Situations you would like to change
Your personal action plan

What exactly is assertiveness?

Assertiveness is a form of behaving in a mature way in a difficult situation. It's a way of communicating how we feel about a situation and what we want to happen. In order to do this we have to be clear ourselves. We have to know how we feel and know what we want to happen. We have to give the other person a chance of saying what he or she feels and what he wants to happen. We have to tell the other person that whilst we understand his position, we still know what we want to happen. By being clear about where we stand, we are more able to discuss the issue and reach a joint agreement.

Assertiveness is built on four pillars:

1. *Self-esteem*: feeling good about yourself.

2. *Self-knowledge*: asking yourself how you feel about a situation, and what you would like to happen.

3. *Respect for others*: listening carefully to the other person, his feelings and his needs.

4. *Clear communication*: telling that person that you understand what he feels and wants, and then telling him clearly what you feel, and what you would like to happen.

This is a formula for resolving both difficult and not so difficult situations. Sometimes you will get exactly what you want, sometimes you won't, and at other times you will agree a compromise. Whichever way it works out, you will have avoided aggressive conflict or being treated like a door mat.

Why be assertive?

Have you ever had angry abuse from a neighbour? Experienced trouble with your relatives putting pressure on you? Wanted to complain about something in a shop? Wondered if it were possible to end a relationship differently? Wished you had made a better impression at an interview?

Life is full of situations like these, where we wish we had

acted in a different way or said what we really thought. Sometimes we keep quiet because we're scared to speak up, sometimes it's because we're confused, often it's because we don't feel confident or perhaps we fear being disliked. For whatever reason, if we haven't said what we thought, and felt, then we will continue to feel angry and upset with ourselves and will dread a similar encounter in the future.

Of course, we don't all act in the same way. Not everyone is intimidated or finds it difficult to speak out. Perhaps you are the sort of person who does speak your mind very easily. Perhaps you don't suffer fools gladly and do raise your voice if things aren't done the way you like. You probably appear very confident, even if people think you are a bit intimidating. Maybe you don't care if you're liked or disliked, but do sometimes regret having bitten someone's head off, or having been sarcastic to an individual who 'just isn't in your league'.

Do you ever wonder if there are other ways of behaving and achieving things?

In situations like these, being assertive will give you the confidence to behave in new ways and establish more equal relationships with people.

Being assertive will help you to:

- handle difficult situations and difficult people

- become more self-confident

- understand more about yourself, your needs and your rights

- tell people what you would like to happen instead of always doing what they want

- feel better for having expressed your feelings

- gain the respect of other people so that they know where they are with you

- balance your needs with those of others.

Behaviour: fight, flight or communication

We all use different behaviour at various times. We have an instinctive FLIGHT (Passive) or FIGHT (Aggressive) reaction to many difficult situations. You've seen people reacting when the fight breaks out in the pub at closing time. Some people will dive for cover, others will be straight into the middle of it all. But there is another way of acting which is based on COMMUNICATION (Assertive). This relies heavily on discussion, negotiation and compromise and is a much more civilised and mature way of behaving. It's rather like the publican who intervenes, calms down the aggressor and manages to bring order to what could be a very destructive and nasty situation.

Behave yourself

You can probably remember being told as a child 'Behave yourself'. This may have been because you weren't getting what you wanted and were having a tantrum, fighting or sulking. At other times you would be encouraged to adopt a more positive kind of behaviour – 'Don't be shy, speak up' or

'Take your fingers out of your mouth'. You were being encouraged to be more independent and to act in a more assertive way.

Even when we are adults, our childish behaviour still lurks beneath the surface. We shout, have rows (Aggressive) or quietly sulk or simmer with resentment if things don't go our way (Passive). Sometimes we resort to using emotional blackmail to get what we want or use our possessions or financial power to our advantage (Manipulative). Watch how children use various negative forms of behaviour to try to get what they want.

As adults there usually isn't anyone there to say 'Behave yourself', so we have to take responsibility for our own behaviour. When you do manage to be assertive and achieve your aims, you feel a satisfaction in your power of communication and your growing independence.

In the next section you will have the chance to look at your behaviour and its effect on other people, the way others behave towards you and your response. You will decide what you would like to change. You will begin to understand how the patterns of your childhood behaviour, often based on fear and bullying, can be broken and transformed by adopting an individual and mature style based on assertiveness.

Different ways of behaving

We talk about people behaving Aggressively, Passively or Assertively.

What does this mean to you?

Try and think of occasions when you have used aggressive or passive or assertive behaviour.

Do you remember what effect it had on others?

Do you remember how you felt about acting that way?

There is space on the next pages for you to write down some of these experiences.

Think about an occasion when you behaved aggressively and write it down.
For example, I can remember how a few years ago I threw a cup of tea at the wall in reaction to a difficult teenager!

Write down your experience.

_____

_____

_____

Choose three words or phrases to describe how you felt at the time.
For instance, I felt angry, provoked, out of control.

1_____

2_____

3_____

Describe the reaction you got from other people.
In my case, there was a shocked silence from the teenager.

_____

_____

_____

Think about an occasion when you behaved passively and write it down.
I remember keeping quiet when someone was criticised unfairly in an office meeting. Afterwards I was very angry and ashamed of myself.

Write down your experiences.

_____

_____

_____

What reaction did you get from other people?
In my case none. Nobody knew.

_____

_____

_____

_____

_____

Think about a situation when you behaved assertively and write it down.
I remember the parent/teachers meeting where I spoke up for the first time.

Write down your experience.

_____

_____

_____

_____

_____

What reaction did you get from other people?
I got applause!

_____

_____

_____

_____

_____

_____

Assertiveness and you

Making positive changes to your behaviour will alter your relationships. Think of some situations where behaving differently would be an advantage. For example, in an office meeting, starting to say what you think might make people notice you; dealing with unsolicited phone calls from double-glazing salesmen would save you time. Think of things you could *start* doing, and things you want to *stop* doing. Include simple things as well as important ones. Small successes give you confidence to move on to bigger things.

At a recent workshop I ran, one woman decided to stop apologising for things at work which were not her fault. Later, she wrote to tell me that she had managed to do this and, as a result, felt much more confident in her ability to tackle bigger issues. After a near miss with a pedestrian, a male colleague has decided to stop cutting in on every other driver in sight. He says he feels much more relaxed and in control.

Write down your changes.

I would like to stop _____

_____

_____

Because _____

_____

_____

I would like to start _____

_____

_____

Because _____

_____

_____

Feeling different

Look at the examples you have written down and imagine how you will feel if you manage to achieve the first aim. Write down that feeling. Think about the second one and so on. For example: If I stop biting my nails I will feel that I look better and that will make me feel more confident.

For example: If I manage to say 'I'd like time to think things over', I feel it will be easier to decide what I really want to do.

If I stop _____

_____

_____

I will feel _____

_____

_____

_____

If I start _____

_____

_____

_____

I will feel _____

_____

_____

_____

Changing your behaviour and becoming more assertive does make you feel different. It increases self-confidence and self-esteem. As you progress through the book and the exercises try to stop every so often and allow some time to think about how you feel.

Thinking about yourself

Being assertive makes you think about yourself more, but not in a selfish way. As you behave assertively you are likely to become a more confident, independent and interesting person. You will begin to:

● feel good about yourself

● acknowledge the things you're good at doing

● rate yourself

● accept praise and handle cricitism

● believe in yourself

● take responsibility for yourself

● ask for what *you* want

● allow yourself to make mistakes, and change your mind

● recognise your responsibility towards others.

Feeling good

Perhaps it's a long time since anyone paid you a compliment. But perhaps it's even longer since you paid yourself one. Compliments acknowledge your good points. Everyone is a mix of good and not so good; assertiveness helps you to accept yourself as a whole person.

Exercise: Paying Yourself a Compliment Take five minutes to think about yourself. Write down a list of your good points. It can be as simple as, 'Being bald is quite sexy' or, 'I'm a good neighbour'. Think of something that makes you feel good about yourself, no matter how small. On one course I ran, I remember a young mother almost in tears saying, 'I'm no good at anything. I'm fat and I look a real mess'. We all waited while she continued to look very miserable. Eventually she said, 'Would it be all right to say I have a nice smile?' Her 'nice smile' was evident quite a lot from that point on.

My compliments to me:

1 _____

_____

_____

2 _____

_____

_____

3 _____

_____

_____

1. Read back what you have written about yourself.

2. Go to the mirror, look at yourself and say them out loud.

3. Over the next few weeks try to find more things you like about yourself. Add them to the list, and say them out loud.

Your rights

Assertiveness recognises that individuals, no matter how imperfect, have rights. That includes you. Sometimes you may forget this and think that other people's rights are more important than yours. They're not.

Remember your rights are equal to everyone else's. I've started a list of rights. You will probably find others you would like to add.

- I have the right to be me.
- I have the right to be treated as an equal.
- I have the right to to ask for what I want.
- I have the right to an opinion.
- I have the right to disagree.
- I have the right to be wrong.
- I have the right to say 'I don't understand'.
- I have the right to make decisions.
- I have the right to express my feelings.
- I have the right to be independent.
- I have the right to choose.
- I have the right to be assertive.
- I have the right _____
- I have the right _____
- I have the right _____
- I have the right _____
- I have the right _____
- I have the right _____
- I have the right _____

Using your head: knowing what you want

Exercising our rights means knowing what we want. Being vague causes misunderstandings and confusion. Unless we take time to think about what we actually want, it will be difficult for us to tell someone else. For instance, if your hairdresser cuts your hair too short. Before you see him again think about how you feel and what you want. On your next visit you will be able to tell him clearly about it. You would say, 'I felt that you cut my hair too short last time. I'd like it left longer please'. If you say 'I wasn't very happy', that is too vague and he won't know what you want. Be specific. It's also easier to refuse other people's requests or ideas if *you know* what *you* want. If you're unclear, you'll find yourself giving in to other people's clear demands, and then you'll feel resentful afterwards.

●

Assertiveness helps you to identify what your needs are

●

Some situations arise unexpectedly and need a quick reaction, but others can be foreseen. Taking time to think about what you want out of expected situations will help you to be more prepared for surprise ones.

In the exercise on the next page there's space to write down some situations which you can anticipate and which you would like to change. Start with something simple. Write down the situation and then write how you feel about it and what you would like to happen. For example: I'm always the last to see the Sunday newspapers because everyone else grabs them . . . I always have to drive my brother and sister-in-law home when they come to visit . . . Why can't someone else think about buying cat food?

A. The situation

_____

_____

B. Write down how you feel about it.
For example: I feel taken for granted, I would rather go to bed than drive them home.

I feel _____

_____

_____

C. Write down what you would like to happen.
For example: I want to read the newspaper when it arrives. I would like them to arrange their own transport home.

_____

_____

_____

Now think about an even more difficult situation you'd like to change. (If even thinking about it makes you feel sick and worried just write it down anyway. Come back to it when you feel ready.)

A. Write down the situation

_____

_____

_____

B. Write down how you feel about it.

_____

_____

_____

C. Write down what you would like to happen.

_____

_____

_____

_____

You have just learnt to be assertive with yourself by using your head to:

● identify what the problem is

● identify how you feel

● identify what you want to happen.

Identifying situations where there are problems is a part of behaving assertively. Deciding when to do something about them is up to you. However, deciding to put assertiveness into practice means being able to tell people very clearly how you feel and what you want.

Communication: finding the right words

You will need to think carefully about the *words*, and how you are going to communicate with the other person. You need to choose simple words which will be easily understood. Here are some guidelines.

1. Choose simple words.

2. Choose words which say what you feel and think.

3. Choose words which say what you want to happen.

4. Choose words which show willingness to discuss things.

Words have to tell someone exactly what is wanted. If you're trying to get a job done it's no good saying to a workman, 'Maybe you can come over *sometime*.' You have to say, 'I'd like you to come over *tomorrow*.'

In Column 1 below there is a list of imprecise words and phrases.

In Column 2 there is space for you to write down more precise, alternative words to those used in Column 1.

To complete this exercise, look at the imprecise words below. Imagine a situation in which you might use them (like organising the workman). Think of precise words to use instead, which make it clear exactly what you want.

Find a precise word for the following:

IMPRECISE	PRECISE
sometime	e.g. *tomorrow*
smallish	e.g. *4 centimetres*
I can't decide	e.g. *I'd like a blue one*
nice	
whenever	
perhaps	
sort of	
pleasant	
I feel fine	
I'm OK	
don't really know	
could you do something about it	
any old thing will do	

Start to include precise, clear words and phrases in your vocabulary. In other words, don't rely on mind readers – there aren't too many of them around!

Note down any imprecise words you use frequently:

_____

_____

_____

_____

The EBBOM factor

We have a phrase in our family, known as the EBBOM factor: 'Engage brain before opening mouth'. It really concentrates the mind and helps you to say what you mean. Try to use EBBOM before you tell someone how you feel about things. Even a moment's quick reflection in a surprise situation will pay off.

Ways of using words

It's not just words and phrases themselves which are powerful, but the way they are said. You can appear Aggressive, Passive or Assertive by your delivery.

Listen to yourself Are there any particular phrases which you wish you didn't use? Do you end your statements with a question as though you want someone's approval or confirmation? Do you apologise before you say what you think? Do you sound hesitant before you make a statement? Does your tone of voice ever seem rude or abrasive?

Tone of voice You can convey all sorts of meanings just by using a different tone, pitch, volume or emphasis. Try saying 'I'd like some help' in as many different ways as you can think of. Listen carefully to your voice as you speak, and also think about how you are feeling as you imagine each situation. Here are some suggested ways to do it:

1. Imagine you are saying it to your family, who are watching television. You are angry because you've been working hard all day and no one has offered to help you prepare the evening meal.

2. Try it as if you were dealing with your boss at work – a person who always makes you feel small and insignificant.

3. Try it as if you were asking someone who won't help anyway – a person at work who is always busy doing something else. You'll probably find a sarcastic edge in your voice.

4. Now try it as if you were talking to a good friend, someone you like and respect and who is usually very willing to offer assistance.

Experimenting with other words or phrases in the same way (try 'Really' or 'I'd like to speak to you') will demonstrate how by changing the tone of your delivery, words can be made to have a different meaning. You can appear snobbish, angry, hurt, bored, interested or sympathetic just by opening your mouth.

Using a cassette recorder Hearing the actual sound of your voice can be helpful. Try repeating this exercise with a cassette recorder. It may sound odd listening to your own voice, but don't worry, we all think our voice sounds strange when we hear it for the first time. The point of using a tape recorder is for you to hear how the meaning of the words changes when you use different tones of voice. Try using your own words and phrases. You will be amazed how much control you can gain over your voice once you start to experiment. You can begin to train it to do what you want.

An assertive voice gets results Take the example of asking for help from a friend. Say the words again. Notice how your voice is quite different from the sarcastic or angry voice used in other situations. It's probably an open and friendly voice, a voice that feels confident in asking a friend for some help, an assertive voice which will probably get the help it's asking for. There's a reason for this. In a relationship where you feel equal you don't anticipate problems. If your friend says 'No, sorry, I'm busy', you don't take it as a sign that you are a failure, incompetent, thoroughly unlovable and disliked by everyone. So why should you react differently to other people like your aggressive boss or your manipulative family? *You* don't change. You are just the same person, and you are just as equal with them as you are with your friend. (Look back to page 24 and Your Rights.)

Breathing properly

Very often when we are anxious we tend to breathe quickly and shallowly. The words come out in a rush and get lost. The other person may not be able to understand what we are trying to say. Breathing well will help to make sure that the words come out clearly, in a strong and assertive manner. It will also calm you down when you're feeling anxious or even angry.

Try this short exercise and feel the difference:
Take a couple of minutes just to think about your breathing. Sit upright and breathe normally. Concentrate on breathing through your nose and filling your lungs. Let the breath out slowly. Take a deeper breath and feel your lungs and your rib-cage really expand. Now try breathing out gently through your mouth. Practise this exercise for about one minute. Repeating it once or twice a day will develop your lungs and will help you to deliver your words in a much stronger way. If you forget to breathe properly you will quickly get breathless, and will appear over-excited and out of control. (This exercise is useful going into any situation which makes you feel nervous, for example an interview or speaking in public. It's also useful in everyday situations when you need to feel calm and confident.)

Trying it out

Exercise: Take what you have written on pages 26–7 and read it out loud. Listen carefully to yourself saying what *you* feel about something and what *you* want to happen. The words may not be quite right yet, but the message is there. This may be quite a surprise. Perhaps you've never thought about what you wanted in this way before. Maybe you'd rather have a quiet life and it all sounds a bit selfish anyway. At this point remind yourself that you won't always get what you want, because most of life is a compromise, and in any case being assertive is also about understanding the other person's needs as well.

Try reading it again.

Exercise: Take the two issues that you described in the exercise on pages 26–7 and write in very simple language what you would say to the person about how you feel and what you want.

For example: 'John, we love seeing you and Mary every Friday, but some weeks I feel very tired and don't feel like driving you home afterwards. Could you arrange some other means of transport for at least one night a month?'

1 _____

_____

_____

_____

_____

2 _____

_____

_____

_____

It probably feels good to have written that, even if you think you'll never be able to say it. Don't worry about this for the moment. It is a very important step to be able to see what the problem is and to have worked out clearly how you feel and what you want. Now you have found the words to express all these things. You are making very good progress.

Perhaps there are other situations which you could decide to tackle in the same way. Remember, you aren't deciding to take action yet. Just look at the problems while you are in a safe place and feel secure.

Practising in private Practising is important. If you don't want other people to overhear you the bathroom is a good place, and there's usually a mirror for you to look into, as well. Start with what you wrote down in the previous exercise.

1. Relax. You know what you feel and what you want.

2. Read out the words in a calm and confident way.

3. Listen carefully to the words.

Ask yourself:

● How does it feel to have said this out loud?

● Imagine what the person it's intended for might say or do.

● If they were angry what would you do?

● If they were upset how would you react?

● What you would say to their reaction?

Stay calm and think how you would restate your case. Look in the mirror. Imagine you are telling that person that you understand their feelings, but still want this to happen.

Congratulations! You have just learned to be assertive with yourself.

You have used your head to:

● think about the problem

● work out how you feel

● work out what you want.

You have used your voice to:

● say what the problem is

● say how you feel about it

● say what you want to happen.

You have begun to:

● think about the other person's feelings and needs

● restate your feelings and say what you want to happen.

Communication: body language

Whatever words we choose, we must look as though we mean them. Speaking is only one part of communicating. We need to support the words with strong body language. Body language is the name given to the non-verbal, almost unnoticed gestures which all of us make all the time, the signs and signals which subtly communicate how we are feeling. Body language has acquired something of a mystique and yet it is something which everyone uses automatically every day.

Just as we learnt as children how to recognise when someone was in a good or bad mood (picking up vibes), so we learn how to interpret the signs of trouble brewing in the workplace or home: it's easy to see someone is angry even before he or she says a word, just by the facial expression or the way he bursts through the door, while someone who approaches you with a smile and gives you a warm handshake conveys confidence and ease.

The more you develop your skills in interpreting other people's body language, and, more importantly, learn how to control and understand your own, the more likely you are to get your message across. Your body language says a lot about you to other people. You can use it to reinforce your message. It too can be Aggressive, Passive or Assertive.

Interpreting and using body language

The chart on page 35 will give you some clues as to how we interpret the way people behave. Look at the Assertive column particularly. These are the habits you want to develop.

Aggressive body language alienates people. It suggests that the person is not comfortable with what he's saying and raises doubts about his message.

Passive body language fails to engage people. It suggests a lack of self-confidence. It weakens the message.

Assertive body language makes people feel confident. It suggests an understanding of the situation and knowledge of what is wanted. It reinforces the message.

	ASSERTIVE	AGGRESSIVE	PASSIVE
Appearance	Relaxed	Tense	Apprehensive
Posture	Upright	Domineering	Collapsed
Eye contact	Direct	Staring	Minimal
Facial expression	Responsive	Taut	Fawning
Hands	Relaxed	Agitated	Limp
Voice	Confident	Strident	Hesitant

Which type of body language do you use most frequently? Write down anything which you'd like to change about it.

I'd like to stop _____

_____

_____

_____

I'd like to improve my _____

_____

_____

_____

_____

_____

We use all three types of body language in varying degrees. When we're going to tackle a difficult situation or confront a difficult person, we can use the non-verbal message to our advantage. If we appear controlled and communicative (assertive) we are much more likely to be listened to than if we appear to be in a rampaging rage or unsure of ourselves.

Involving a partner

If you have a supportive partner or friend it's a good idea to involve him or her in your assertiveness. Always choose someone you feel safe with. Explain that you are trying to learn to be more assertive and deal with some particular problems. Ask for help. If you involve the other person, he or she is less likely to feel threatened in any way, so it will have all sorts of benefits.

Your partner could start by pointing out any mannerisms (body language) which you may not be aware of. Then you could move on to role play.

Role play

This is a useful way of rehearsing what you might want to say or do in a particular situation. Start off with something simple which will give you an idea of how useful role play can be. For example, you might imagine being in a restaurant where your food has been over-cooked. You dread the thought of complaining in public, but realise that sometimes you wish you were able to do this. You play the part of the customer and your partner plays the role of the restaurant manager. You then behave as though the situation were real. Try to handle the situation assertively, and ask your partner to respond to your behaivour. You will find yourselves quickly identifying with each role.

At first you may feel a little silly or self-conscious but this will quickly vanish as you find that you are not 'acting', but are responding naturally to what is happening. You will experience the feelings of indignation, guilt, frustration and disappointment which would be normal in such a situation. Try it out for yourself.

Role play can be a helpful way of seeing how we behave in difficult situations, and understanding the effect of our behaviour on other people.

Try swapping roles – you play the restaurant manager and see what it feels like to be in his shoes. In later chapters we will look at the use of role play when dealing with difficult problems and relationships.

This is one example. Now think of some other situations for yourself.

- Role play allows you to practice changing your behaviour.

- Role play is a safe way of finding out what reactions you will get to a change in your behaviour.

- Role play lets you experience another person's feelings.

- Role play is a way of defusing your emotions.

Remember the Assertiveness Guidelines:

● Say what you feel

● Say what you want

● Suggest the action to be taken

● Listen to the response

● Restate your case

● Try to reach an amicable agreement.

Feedback

Understanding how our words and actions sound to someone else is important. A partner can give you this feedback,
for example, after a role play session. It should be an honest
appraisal of your performance. Before giving or receiving
feedback read the guidelines below.

Guidelines for receiving feedback:

1. You must want to receive the comments.

2. Choose someone you trust.

3. Be prepared for criticism, and to accept it if you think it is
correct.

4. If you don't agree, don't argue about it. Remember you
asked your partner to comment on your behaviour, and now
he or she is telling you. It is the truth as your partner sees it.
Remember your partner is trying to help you.

5. You do *not* have to accept everything that is said. If you
don't think the comments are right then if possible check it
out with someone else later.

6. Always thank your partner.

7. Even if you don't like what you heard, remember this is
probably the first time someone has been this truthful with

you. It gives you an enormous amount of new information. You can choose to use it if you want to.

Giving feedback (partner to read this):

1. Comment on the *behaviour* – this avoids criticism becoming too personal or hurtful. For example: 'I felt your behaviour was too timid', rather than, 'You were awfully timid'.

2. Comment on how appropriate the behaviour was to the particular situation you were dealing with. For example, 'That felt a bit too strong, perhaps you could try a gentler approach'.

3. Suggest ways of improving the impression given. This could include words, tone of voice, eye contact and body language.

Putting it into practice

● You've learnt how to use your head

● You've learnt how to use your body

● You've discovered which problems are troubling you

● You've worked out which words to use

● You're tried using your voice

● You've tried practising on your own

● You've probably done some role play

● You may have had some feedback.

Caution You have not as yet had any practice in a real situation. Just because you can manage a role play session doesn't mean you can take on the world.

Start with something small You know enough now for you to feel quietly confident that it is probably possible to change one small thing. Take a few minutes to think about it. If you can't decide what it will be now, think about it over the next few days.

Taking the initiative

A good assertive start to any problem is for *you* to take the initiative. If *you* are raising the issue, *you* are in the driving seat. You will know what you want to say and will even think of some of the words to use. This is your opportunity for you to say what you want to happen. Starting the discussion gives you an advantage because you choose the terms on which the conversation takes place.

Choose the right moment Some people will do all this hard work and then will ruin it by trying to raise an issue at an inappropriate time. Starting a conversation with a football-mad son just as coverage of the day's big match is beginning is guaranteed to fail. If your husband has had a dreadful time at work don't raise the subject of sharing the housework as he sits down. If you want to complain about the behaviour of someone at work, make sure that there is time and space for the conversation. Nothing is worse than the other person saying, 'Sorry, I haven't got the time now, I have to be somewhere in five minutes'. You lose the initiative, and feel put down again. Choose the time and the place carefully whenever you can.

●

Assertiveness builds self-respect

●

Techniques for dealing with other people's reactions

Even with the clearest message people sometimes just don't want to know. You may find the other person isn't listening, or may become aggressive towards you. It's at this point that *you* need still to be in control. Remember:

1. Make your message clear.

2. Be persistent.
You may have to try communicating your message several times on different occasions. Be persistent and patient, making it clear that you feel strongly about the situation and you want something doing.

3. Repeat the message.
There is a technique called the 'Broken Record' which is useful when someone refuses to act. For example, if you have taken something back to a shop which is clearly faulty and the assistant refuses to exchange it, you can sometimes get action by repeating your original point, for example 'The goods are faulty and I want a refund'. If she refuses to co-operate, acknowledge that you have heard what she has said, continue to stand your ground and repeat, 'The goods are faulty and I want a refund'. This is often successful because you refuse to alter your position, regardless of what she says or does, and continue to repeat your message clearly.

4. Stay cool.
People will react to you in different ways. If they become argumentative or aggressive, stay calm and clear about what you want. Remember, it's not worth allowing yourself to become upset over the situation. If things become nasty, retain your feelings of self-worth by keeping a cool head. You can always come back to discuss it another day.

5. Keep to the issue.
Some people will try 'fogging' the issue by dragging in other, irrelevant, ones. For example, if a colleague has been very aggressive to you in a meeting, you might take him on one

side later and say, 'I feel that your behaviour was unnecessarily aggressive today. Please don't speak to me again like that.' He might respond with ,'You might think I was aggressive to you in the meeting but I think you look awful today'. By turning to the question of your appearance he is completely fogging the issue. Don't be side-tracked. Deal briskly with it and restate your case. 'John, you may be right and I don't look wonderful today, but we're talking about the way you behaved in the meeting. I feel very angry about it and I don't want you to speak to me again like that.'

6. Work out solutions.
Don't forget you are looking for joint solutions to the problem. Other examples of these techniques are given in the following chapters. In particular, we'll look at how they work in different relationships.

At this point it is worth repeating the advice given earlier. You now have an enormous amount of very valuable knowledge. You can transform some of the more problematic relationships in your life. Do it gradually.

Situations you would like to change

Think of examples of situations which you would like to resolve: the way you always say 'Yes' when people ask to borrow things; a long-standing row with a neighbour; a work situation which needs improving; a difficult family problem.

You don't necessarily have to complete the list now. New situations are sure to crop up which you may like to add: you may encounter new and even more difficult workmen; you may get phone calls from insurance salesmen; your neighbours may buy a noisy dog.

Over the next few months you can come back and look at your list. As your confidence grows you can decide to do something about the issues. You may never sort them all out, but seeing them written down will feel like a good first step to being assertive.

Now make your own list of those situations you would like to change.

1 _____

_____

_____

_____

2 _____

_____

_____

_____

3 _____

_____

_____

_____

4 _____

_____

_____

_____

5 _____

_____

_____

_____

6 _____

_____

_____

_____

Your Personal Action Plan

Think about this chapter. What was the most important thing you learned? *Write it down.*

_____

_____

_____

_____

Start and stop

Think of a way of behaving which would help you to feel more assertive. Decide to *start* using it. (It may be as simple as deciding to say which television programmes you want to see.) Then think of something in your behaviour which stops you from feeling assertive. Decide to *stop* doing it. (For example, it could be as simple as stopping yourself from akways apologising before you say something that really matters to you.)

On the opposite page there is an Action Plan for you to fill in. Be specific. Write down things which you know you can manage to achieve. Write as many things as you want to; there's enough space for you to come back later to add more.

Start with some simple things and enjoy finding out about the new assertive you.

●

Assertiveness helps you to be yourself

●

Action Plan

I am going to start _____

_____

_____

_____

_____

_____

_____

_____

_____

_____

_____

_____

I am going to stop _____

_____

_____

_____

_____

_____

_____

_____

_____

_____

_____

_____

Date _____

CHAPTER TWO

Assertiveness with Family and Friends

OBJECTIVES

To help you to:
- improve family relationships
- improve the way you communicate
- deal with difficult situations at home
- deal with difficult people at home
- encourage others to become assertive
- improve relationships with friends

SUMMARY

The challenge of the family
Why problems arise
Behaviour: aggressive, passive or assertive
Changing things
Your rights as a member of the family
Preparing yourself
Communicating with your family
Tackling problems
Games families play
Establishing adult relationships
Children and assertiveness
Old dogs learning new tricks
Assertiveness and friends
Being assertive in sexual relationships
Your personal action plan

The challenge of the family

Families come in all shapes and sizes. They can be fun and they can be hell. There are times when we may find ourselves wishing we had another family, but, unfortunately, we're saddled with the one we've got. In the circumstances, we can only make the best of it.

'The family' today can include anything from single-parent households to elderly brothers and sisters living together. The typical nuclear family might be declining, but with divorce and re-marriage becoming commonplace families are suddenly extending in new and complex ways. A new partner often brings a package: step-children, a new mother-in-law, step-grandparents, sisters-in-law with husbands and kids who all consider themselves part of 'the family', and who all try to make claims on us.

Families are where we first learn to relate to other people. They are a testing ground for life, offering a relatively safe haven for discovering more about ourselves and more about other people. However, because relationships are so close and because of the peculiar power distributions in them, they can also bring their own problems, particularly ones of communication.

Friends

Many of the things you are about to learn also apply to your behaviour with friends. Later in the chapter we will look specifically at friends and some of the different kinds of relationships we have with them.

Family communication

When members of a family don't communicate with each other, the result can be a nightmare for everyone. Insignificant issues get blown up out of all proportion, people bear grudges, problems are imagined where they don't exist, paranoia develops, resulting in a lot of unhappiness.

Families are human

We often forget that our family consists of real human beings. In order to get what they want, individuals behave in ways which they have used since their childhood: they can be Manipulative, Passive, Aggressive or Assertive.

You may not have had a choice about the family you were born into, but you do have a choice about the way you behave within that family. Behaving assertively is one of those choices.

If people behave assertively in their relationships within the family it can help to avoid an awful lot of unhappiness and misunderstanding. Now that you're learning how to be assertive with yourself the next big task is to turn your attention to your family.

Behaving assertively

Assertiveness within the family group is no different from any other kind of assertiveness: take it one small step at a time. Remember, being assertive means that you will change your behaviour patterns. Make it easier on yourself, and your family, by not trying to change too much too quickly, and above all by being clear in what you say.

As you go further on in the book you'll begin to see that what you learn about being assertive with your family will apply to other relationships you have, at work or with neighbours. Although these relationships are different, the same basic guidelines apply.

Saying 'No'

Families surround us, invade our space, make demands on us and love us. We find ourselves agreeing to do something because it's someone in the family who has asked and it's impossible to refuse. We can't possibly refuse – or can we? Behaving assertively means having more confidence to turn down some of these manipulative requests. Saying 'No' to persistent relatives may be difficult if you've always said 'Yes'. Start by asking yourself, 'What do *I* really want?'.

Assertiveness for all the family

Whatever our age we are never too old and never too young to learn how to improve our assertiveness skills. Introducing assertiveness to every generation of the family is like giving them a dose of medicine for their common ailments: manipulation, tantrums, sulks, anger, fights, blackmail and threats. The improvement is quite dramatic.

Later in the chapter we will look at assertiveness and different family age groups; from grandparents to children.

Breaking old habits The habits of behaviour learnt in childhood often last well into adulthood when it comes to getting what we want from those we love. Within the family framework it's particularly easy for us to remain locked into those attitudes and behaviours which we used as a child. If we always got what we wanted as a child by bullying, then we still use this behaviour when we want something now.

Assertiveness will help you to break the old childish habits and adopt more adult ones. Assertiveness is about growing up in the way you behave and deal with people, particularly in your family.

Not liking everyone It is perfectly all right not to like all the members of your family. We accept that we do not like all the people we come across in our lives, so it is rather unrealistic to think that somehow we should like all this 'family of individuals' we acquire when we are born. Very often, though, it's people's behaviour that we don't like. By being assertive we bring the possibility of change to the situation.

When my children were small and misbehaved I would say to them, 'I don't *like* you at all when you behave like that. I still love you, but I don't like you behaving that way and I'm not prepared to put up with it.' In the same way we have to convey this message in the same assertive way to adult, manipulative relatives: we don't like them when they behave this way, and we have no intention of putting up with it any longer. This doesn't mean we love them any the less.

Why problems arise

Problems in families are caused by three things:

1. You

2. Difficult people

3. Difficult situations.

You Taking responsibility for our behaviour is all part of being assertive. Probably some of our worst behaviour is with family. In other relationships we may try to hide our weaknesses, whereas in the family we often don't bother.

Blaming other people When things go wrong there is a tendency in families to blame other people. Accepting our part in the problem, taking responsibility and looking for solutions are all part of being assertive. Blaming other people is not the answer.

Difficult people Even the perfect family will usually admit to having one or two members, maybe distant cousins, with whom they have difficulties. Dealing with any difficult person is always hard. When you add on family pressure as well it's no wonder that most of us just give up and either have blazing rows or take a passive line. The alternative is to try using your new assertiveness skills.

Difficult situations A combination of 'You, Other Difficult Family Members and a Situation' can lead to enormous problems. Emotions in families run high. Unlike problems at work or in the community, you can't walk away from them. It's not unusual for other long-forgotten issues to be dredged up. Even if the immediate situation is quite small, the surrounding tensions rapidly build up.

Whether it's a small issue like who's job is it to buy the toilet rolls, or a more serious and complex issue like giving up a job in order to look after an elderly relative, what is needed is a cool head and clear communication.

Behaviour: aggressive, passive or assertive

People behave very differently in the different segments of their lives. A hesitant, unassuming person who would never think of disagreeing with the family at home may become a tyrant at work. You've seen how your behaviour can change, how you can be supremely confident and assertive in one sphere and timid and tongue-tied in another. Let's look at how you behave with your family, how you see yourself and how you think your family sees your behaviour.

Your behaviour

The way your family treat you will have quite a lot to do with the way you behave towards them. They will have formed an impression of you, which you have reinforced every day of your life, since you were a child, by your responses to events. Even if you are now an adult you may still resort to childish behaviour from time to time, particularly with close members of your family. Think about particular incidents where you have perhaps had a disagreement with a brother or sister. How often do you find yourself echoing the phrases you used when you had fights as children. 'Oh, you always behave like that' or, 'I knew you'd say that'. How often do you back down, swear or go into sulk?

In the next few exercises you will have the chance to look closely at your behaviour and decide if there are things you want to change. Be absolutely honest with yourself.
Five things to think about:

1. *Your view of you* – how you see yourself in the family

2. *Your family's view of you* – how others see your behaviour

3. *Your feelings* – how you feel about your family role

4. *Your actions* – how you behave in family situations

5. *Family communication* – how you communicate with the rest of your family.

Your view of you

In the last chapter you discovered how to build up your confidence and self-esteem. When dealing with your family, self-esteem is even more important. If you play the part of the drudge, door mat or long-suffering individual, you will find that your family are only too happy to support you in the 'victim' role. It may be useful at this stage to refer back to the questionnaire on pages 10–12.

Assessing yourself How do you behave when you deal with other members of the family?
– Are you passive, aggressive or assertive?
– Are you the leader of the family?
– Are you the one people turn to when there's a problem?
– The one who always gets the rotten jobs?
– The one who tries to please everyone?
– The one who worries, but says little?

Describe your behaviour Here are some words which might describe your behaviour when you deal with your family. See if you think any apply to you.

- Argumentative   (aggressive)
- Efficient   (assertive)
- Macho   (aggressive)
- Timid   (passive)
- Honest   (assertive)
- Impatient   (aggressive)
- Critical   (aggressive and/or assertive)
- Apologetic   (passive)
- Indecisive   (aggressive and/or passive)

Add any others which you think are appropriate:

_____

_____

_____

By now you should be getting an idea of how you think you behave with your family. All behaviour is a mix but on balance you will probably find that there is one type of behaviour to which you constantly resort. Consider how this behaviour affects the others.

Your family's view of you

What have your family come to expect of your behaviour? What do they think of you? Sometimes the answers are very different from the image you have of yourself.

Descriptions of you? Look at the following chart and see if any of the phrases are ones which your family might use about you.

AGGRESSIVE	PASSIVE	ASSERTIVE
She'll just sulk.	He's no use in a crisis.	Let's ask her; she always has good suggestions.
Don't tell him. He'll just rake up the past and get personal.	Don't worry, she'll agree.	He'll want to hear everyone's views before he decides.
He'll say he's no intention of changing his holiday plans at this stage.	She'll have Mum to stay for Christmas. Just tell her you're going ski-ing.	She'll want us to discuss things and share the responsibility.
She still terrifies me.	She was always a cry baby as a child.	She has always shared things, even when we were little.

Feedback If you want to find out how your behaviour appears to others, ask someone you trust for his or her opinion. (Have a look at the guidelines on feedback in Chapter 1, page 38.)

Explain what you are doing and ask your partner if your view is one that he or she agrees with. Look at the chart together. Does he or she agree with what you think about yourself?

Listen even if you don't like what you hear. You don't have to accept what is said, but it is how it seems to your partner, so it is still a valuable opinion.

Your feelings Behaving assertively means being aware of your feelings. In all dealings with your family allow yourself the space to ask, 'How do I feel about this?' Remember, *your* rights as a member of the family are equal to other people's.

Changing things

We've all heard people say, 'He was acting quite out of character'. Often this is said when a person has done something quite unexpected and has changed both his behaviour pattern and a situation.

A good example of this was the famous French painter Gauguin who was married with five children. He lived a boring suburban life as a bank manager. One day at the age of 35 he left his wife and children and vanished to become a painter, eventually ending up living with the Polynesian Islanders. No doubt his family revised their opinion of him.

Many of us live for years with situations which we would like to change. Using assertiveness to discover what we feel about situations and what we want to happen, may help us to find ways of resolving some of these problems.

Major decisions, affecting other people, are not easy to make. Before deciding on any action, think the situation through carefully. Ask yourself what you feel. Only when you are clear about what you want to do, and have the strength to tackle the problem, is it time to act.

In my case, after 15 years of marriage, I finally had the

courage to do what I felt was right and I left my husband. Making that decision was not easy, particularly since we had three children. I'm sure my family and a lot of other people thought I was acting out of character. I had, after all, been a 'dutiful daughter', before becoming the 'perfect wife and mother'. Assertiveness can bring enormous and liberating life-changes, but should always be used carefully. Remember, having rights means having responsibilities too.

How will people react?

Most changes aren't so big, but you still have to be prepared for reactions. If you've worked through Chapter One you will already be beginning to value yourself and your feelings. Having respect for yourself will help you to deal with many of these reactions.

Your family know so much about you that if you make any changes in the way you've always behaved, they won't hesitate to tell you. They may respond to more assertive behaviour with some surprise. They may not know how to deal with it. They may be 'put out' because you aren't doing what you've always done, and they aren't getting what they've always managed to get. On the other hand, they may be delighted to see the difference in you and may react very positively. Your assertiveness could be a pleasant surprise.

Dealing with their reactions is part of the process of assertiveness, and there is no reason why you shouldn't stand back and enjoy watching how different people react.

What will they say?

Probably quite a lot. Families usually do. They criticise, whinge, moan and use every ploy in the book. They also applaud, praise and approve.

Be prepared for jokes, put-downs, personal comments and remarks which only confirm that you have a lot of assertive ground to make up. Don't be put off, and above all don't slip back into your old passive or aggressive habits.

Over the years I've been on the receiving end of some classic comments including:

'You worry me, our Claire, you really do.'
'You've changed your tune!'
'I thought that you cared more about me.'
'Have you ever thought you might be lesbian?'
'You've no right to . . .'
'I don't know where you get these ideas from.'
'You never think of anyone else.'

Most of these responses are aggressive or manipulative (a quiet and devious form of aggressive behaviour). We all allow ourselves to be manipulated from time to time, sometimes with very damaging effects. Don't collude with manipulators.

It can be a simple phrase which will undermine you, particularly if it's delivered by someone you care about. A seemingly simple question can make you stop in your tracks and really agonise. It can make you ask yourself: 'Am I really selfish?', 'Am I being unreasonable in wanting this to happen?' or 'Perhaps they're right and I'm wrong'.

Write down a phrase which 'stops you in your tracks'. Do you know why it has that effect? _____

_____

_____

_____

Positive responses

Expect positive responses to your changed behaviour, too. After years of wanting to make a specific comment and always holding back for fear of upsetting someone, when you finally say it and hear the reply 'I'm so glad you've told me that', or 'I wish I'd known that a long time ago', it's like a rainbow brightening up the day.

Your rights as a member of the family

Whatever your family's reaction to you and your new assertive behaviour, remind yourself that you also have rights as a person and as a member of the family. Exercise those rights – you will feel less like a door mat or a bulldozer and, in time, are likely to win more respect from your family. Here are some of your rights. There is space for you to add other ones which are important for you.

My rights

● I have the right to speak out.

● I have the right to be heard.

● I have the right to be treated as a person, not just as a daughter/wife/mother/son/grandad.

● I have the right to privacy.

● I have the right to disagree.

● I have the right to be consulted and involved.

● I have the right to _____

● I have the right to _____

● I have the right to _____

Remember, these rights apply to *everyone*.

WOOL ALLERGY, LITTLE SIS? SINCE 1923?

Preparing yourself

Assertiveness means being more in control of your life and responding to events in a more confident way. Part of that confidence comes from knowing what you want to change, and working out the best way to do it. It's a good idea to start with small problems first.

Resolving small problems

An unresolved problem can make family life a misery. Whether it's big or small, living with it only makes things worse. It may be the simplest thing which really gets you mad: dirty dishes and half-empty cups of coffee left around; teenagers monopolising the telephone or playing loud music; step-sons who borrow your sweaters; sisters who pinch your tights and make-up. Family life is filled with all kinds of irritating things which can be intensely aggravating if you're not prepared to speak out and say how you feel. You go on putting up with things for all sorts of reasons:

● he/she will be abusive

● saying something may cause more trouble

● I don't want to offend someone

● they're old/sick/depressed/have work problems

● I'll look like a trouble-maker

● I don't really have any right

● what will the rest of the family say?

● they depend on me

● it won't make any difference anyway.

Being assertive means finding the inner strength and confidence to tackle irritating issues. In the last chapter we dealt with techniques which will help. Now is the time to try using some of them.

Communicating with your family

The first thing to remember is that no matter how important the issue is to you, and regardless of the number of sleepless nights you've had worrying about it, unless you tell people clearly what the problem is, they won't understand.

An assertive approach

1. Name the person Say the name of the person(s) you are speaking to. This avoids the family excuse of 'Oh, I thought you were talking to him/her/the cat, etc.'

2. Be specific If you want people to help with the housework then be specific. Don't generalise by saying, 'Nobody ever helps', and then going into a sulk.

3. Say what you feel 'I'm unhappy about the amount of housework that I am having to do.'

4. Say what you would like to happen 'I would like you (all) to help more in the house. I suggest we draw up a rota so that we share things out more fairly.'

5. Discussion and action Try not to leave the resolution till later, otherwise you'll lose the initiative. 'I've got a pen and paper here, let's do it now', you can say.

For example: If you feel that your children, or another member of the household, are always on the telephone and that none of your friends can get through, let alone being able to make phone calls out, then you could say something like:

1. 'Chris and David, I know that your friends phone you, but you are on the phone every night for over 3 hours.'

2. 'This means no one else can receive or make calls. I feel this is unfair; we would all like to use the phone.'

3. 'I want us to decide on a new way of using the phone which is fairer to everybody. I'd like to suggest that your friends call before 8.00 pm (suggest a suitable time) unless it's urgent. I'd

also like you to restrict your outgoing calls to the same time (before 8.00 pm) and make them shorter (specify, say 10 minutes each).'

4. Ask how they feel about it.

5. Listen to what they have to say. (Remember, being assertive means understanding the other person's point of view.)

6. Repeat how you feel and what you want.

7. Agree a joint compromise if necessary.

•

Assertiveness means listening to the other person too

•

Tackling problems

Assertively tackling a small problem

Think of a situation you would like to alter. Perhaps the way you always agree to do something, or other people's behaviour towards you. Identify who the problem is with; it could be one or more people. Write down how you feel about it, using the words 'I feel . . .'. Write down what you would like to happen using the words 'I would like . . .'

Write down the situation _____

_____

_____

_____

_____

Who does it relate to (an individual or a family group)? _____

_____

_____

I feel _____

_____

_____

I would like _____

_____

_____

Think about their reaction. What compromises would you be prepared to make?
Perhaps you're even ready to use that example and try to change that particular situation. Think about it and when it feels right try it out.

Assertively beginning to tackle a big problem

Most of us have at least one big family problem which we find difficulty in resolving. It could be a long-term situation which somehow just developed, or a more recent, but just as complicated, situation which makes you feel sick with worry.

Perhaps you want to leave home and don't know how to broach the subject. Perhaps you want to change your job and daren't tell your family. Perhaps you are old and live alone, and want to see more of your family. *Write it down.*

The problem is _____

_____

I feel _____

_____

_____

I want _____

_____

_____

1. Think about it carefully Work out any reasons why you are waiting to say or do something.

– Are you worried about someone's feelings?

– Are you too shy?

– Are you afraid?

– Are you in awe?

– Are you too angry?

– Do you know what you want?

– Are you waiting for the right moment?

– Is it difficult to find the right opportunity?

2. How do you feel about the situation? If the answer is 'Not very happy with things as they are', then decide what you want to happen. You are probably the only person who can change things. Sometimes that will mean that the other person won't get what he or she wants, but why should you always be the one to make sacrifices and come at the end of the queue?

3. Go slowly. Identifying a problem is a big step in itself By the end of this chapter you will have more ideas for taking assertive action, which will help you to deal with big family problems. Don't rush to use your new-found skills, or be too adventurous too soon. Start with simple issues and build on your successes.

Games families play

All families play games. Most of them are based on power. Individuals use power, manipulation and emotional black-mail, sometimes joining with other family members to exert group pressure on individuals. Standing up to this sort of pressure can be difficult, particularly if it's behaviour which has been used for years.

Power

Your family has a power structure which affects the way everyone behaves. Although you were born into this power structure, you do have the possibility of changing it as you grow up. You may be terrified of your elder brother's temper, perhaps your grandma dominates everything, or your children make unreasonable demands on your time. Assertiveness helps you to deal with different kinds of diffi-cult family behaviour.

Using power well

Power is the key to good family relationships. Using it well creates a more equal environment where everyone has the opportunity to say what he or she feels and wants. This means that problems get resolved quicker. Where does the power lie in your family? Is it your father who lays down the law? Is your mother really the 'power behind the throne'? Where do you fit in?

Mis-using power

Individuals who mis-use and abuse their power cause great unhappiness to other family members: a tyrant of a father may make life hell by demanding that all the family unquestioningly obey him; mothers who are unwilling to 'cut their little boy's apron strings' cause extreme distress to young couples; old people who pretend they are ill cause endless worry to their children.

Mis-use of power is an aggressive form of behaviour. We should not allow ourselves to be involved with it.

Common forms of this behaviour include:

● Emotional – playing on people's feelings

● Physical – using physical strength to win

● Intellectual – using arrogance and put-downs in argument

● Financial – controlling the use of money or promising some material reward.

Abuse of power: emotional blackmail

Most families have experience of one emotional black-mailer. The person uses this particularly nasty kind of aggressive behaviour when he or she want something very badly, and is prepared to resort to manipulative behaviour to get it, for example, 'I'll be left on my own if I can't come to you'. The demands are often unfair, but the individual gets away with it because he knows how to play on our emotions. We feel guilty even at the idea of saying 'No'!

The blackmailer will be clear in his or her selfish expecta-tion that 'family comes first' (meaning him or herself), regardless of others' rights. The truth is that most of us do feel a strong affection and loyalty to our family, but when this is 'used' by individuals in a dishonest way to make us feel guilty, it's time to be assertive.

The guilt trap

Guilt is not a useful emotion. We feel guilty for all sorts of reasons: for letting others down, imagining that we are being selfish or uncaring, wishing we could 'do more'. Sometimes we feel a 'sense of obligation' and fall into a sort of 'compassion trap' towards other family members. We feel we 'have a duty' to do certain things, that we are 'not behaving properly' and so on.

Emotional blackmailers recognise the signs and play on our feelings of guilt. They specialise in increasing this guilt, and try to 'spoil' our pleasure by implying that we obviously 'don't care about them', because if we *really* cared, we would do what *they* want.

Dealing with feelings of guilt

The way to deal with people who try to induce guilt is to be assertive:

1. Know how you feel.

2. Know what you want.

3. State these quite clearly.

4. Listen to what the other person is saying.

5. Reassure him or her that you have heard what he is saying.

6. Repeat what you want to happen.

7. Suggest your compromise and ask for alternatives.

8. Agree a compromise between the two of you.

Be on your guard The person will often end up sighing and saying, 'I suppose I'll just have to put up with it', which is intended to make you feel guilty all over again. Remember, *guilt is a waste of energy.*

Abuse of power: physical

Some people use physical strength to wield power. For anyone who is subjected to this kind of abuse, being assertive is not an easy option. Saying what they feel, let alone what they want to happen, is probably almost impossible when dealing with violent and aggressive family members. Being assertive in a physically threatening environment is very difficult. Violence is something which would hold most people in check. Even reading this book is a great step forward. Remember that many people have eventually faced violent and aggressive bullies, but they have done it in their own time and when it was right for them. Wait until you feel it is the right time for you, before you take any action.

Dealing assertively with physical abuse
1. Try repeating some of the exercises which will build up your belief in your own worth.

2. Remember the exercise in Chapter One where you paid yourself a compliment (page 23). It is well worth repeating this exercise quite frequently.

3. Look for the good qualities in your character which enable you to put up with the violent or aggressive behaviour.

4. If you are in this position, there are groups like the Samaritans who can listen to your problems. For women, there are now many groups which organise assertiveness courses and also offer a supportive atmosphere. Your local library will have lists of addresses.

In the meantime you may find other positive examples, later in the book, of things you might like to tackle, perhaps outside your home. Being more assertive with neighbours or friends might be a good start.

●

Each day pay yourself a compliment

●

Abuse of power: intellectual

We all know the arrogant members of the family who are always trying to impress us with how clever they are. Frequently they resort to 'put downs' which are based on what they see as their superior knowledge. 'Don't you know that?' they say loudly, trying to embarrass you, often in front of other people. This kind of behaviour is aggressive. It makes other people resentful and encourages them either to retaliate aggressively or to hide passively in a corner.

Dealing assertively with intellectual abuse

1. Remember that included in your rights is the right not to know everything.

2. Try saying very calmly, 'No, I don't know that' to Mr Clever Clogs – you may just take the wind out of his sails. Underneath, know-alls are frequently insecure, but this is no excuse for behaviour which is calculated (aggressively) to show their superiority.

Abuse of power: financial and material blackmail

Using money and financial reward to dominate others is another insidious abuse of power. It is a form of aggressive behaviour. It relies on people colluding with the blackmailer for fear they will miss out on hand-outs or find themselves cut out of the family will.

I watched a close relative wait for 20 years for her inheritance from a family business. She and her sisters danced attendance on an old relative, always doing what he wanted, making sure that their children did the same, and never disagreeing with him. He enjoyed the power he had over the family, although he never had their respect. When he died he left everything to a dogs' home.

These situations can go on for years. Everyone becomes locked into them. Nobody knows how to change things. Everyone fears that they will lose out.

Dealing assertively with financial blackmailers

1. Refuse to allow people to manipulate you with rewards.

2. Remind yourself that relationships based on power and dominance have the seeds of destruction within them.

3. Refuse to allow others control over you.

The 'pecking order'

Being assertive with our families helps to protect us from the 'pecking order' which evolves in many families. This is where different members assume a ranking in the family hierarchy. No one dares question these positions, and the quiet, passive types find themselves at the end of the line; the last to be consulted and know what's happening. Being assertive means speaking up at home and saying what *you* want.

Establishing new relationships

Being assertive with our families means establishing adult relationships with all the members, regardless of their chronological age. How often do we treat our elderly parents as if they were small children, or behave like children ourselves when we are with them?

Action

Now it's time to try flexing your assertiveness muscles, and start to change things.

Exercise: Think of a simple situation in your family which you would like to change. Write down what is keeping you from doing something about it. Write down what action you can take.

The situation _____

_____

_____

_____

What is keeping me from doing something? _____

_____

_____

_____

_____

What action can I take? _____

_____

_____

_____

_____

Now think of a more serious situation and write it down.

_____

_____

_____

What is keeping me from doing something? _____

_____

_____

_____

_____

What action can I take? _____

_____

_____

_____

_____

You don't always succeed

Not everybody will respond to assertive behaviour. Sometimes with family problems you feel a bit like a rabbit caught in the headlights, you just get transfixed. I remember going through a period when my son was doing his exams and he refused to get up in the morning. I tried everything, cups of morning coffee, cheery greetings, long discussions, all to no avail. He got up when he was ready and there wasn't anything I could do about it. I have to admit that on a couple of occasions my assertiveness became rather aggressive, and that didn't work either. It's important to remember that assertiveness doesn't always work.

Alternative strategy Exchanging stories and anxieties in a group session, I heard how one family in desperation had 'swapped' their teenage son with a boy from another family who were having similar difficulties. Both boys were consulted and agreeable, and the arrangement lasted for about six months. Both boys found it much easier to communicate with the adults, and both sets of parents found no difficulties in saying what they thought. A quite unusual and clever compromise, and in fact a very assertive one. (Before I could find anyone to swap with my son, he started to get up in the morning, passed his exams and went on to other things.) Both families found it much easier to deal with someone outside their own family group. They treated each other like people and not just as 'family' members.

Assertiveness in the family

- is *not* about having power over someone

- is *not* about 'winning'

- is *not* about dominating others

- *is* about equality

- *is* about your rights.

Children and assertiveness

We should begin to encourage children to be assertive from an early age. They will be happier and more confident. It will also improve communication and help to avoid the misunderstandings that lead to family rows.

Encouraging a child to be assertive means treating him or her as an individual. Helping him to say how he feels, and listening to his views, gives him confidence. If you also teach him to compromise, he will learn that assertiveness means being aware of other people's rights and does not mean always getting what he wants.

Once a child sees that by behaving reasonably (assertively) he is more likely to be listened to, he will be more inclined to act this way. But don't expect miracles overnight. Remember, assertiveness takes time.

Can you think of a situation with a child which could be improved by using assertive behaviour with him or her? Perhaps it's the way clothes are left strewn around, or the way he always walks through the house with muddy boots on. Choose simple things to start with; later you can go on to bigger things. *Write down your example, say what you feel and want to happen.*

The situation _____

_____

I feel _____

_____

_____

What I would like to happen _____

_____

_____

_____

Understanding the adult's standpoint

Sometimes adults appear to have one set of rules for themselves and one for children. In an assertive family, children's opinions are taken into consideration.

If you are a young member of the family, think of a situation you would like to change. Perhaps it's the way your parents insist on what time you come home at night. In this case you could say something like, 'I feel that it's unfair that I always have to come home before my friends. I would like to stay out later. Can we discuss this?'

Write down the situation _____

_____

How I feel _____

_____

What I want to happen _____

_____

_____

More serious problems for children

Victimisation, physical abuse, sexual abuse, saying 'No' to strangers and bullying are all serious problems which children may have to face. Being assertive is part of their defence system and should be encouraged.

Victimisation Maybe you have a child who is being victimised by a teacher at school. Perhaps untrue allegations about the child's behaviour are being made to the head teacher or other members of staff. From experience, I know a child will be devastated by unfair treatment of this kind. Victimisation is a way of aggressively denying someone his rights. Children should be encouraged to recognise this and given the moral support to behave as assertively as they can in what is a very difficult situation.

Saying 'No' A child who feels confident of his or her rights and who has a strong feeling of his own self-worth is much more likely to find the inner strength to stand up for himself against potential abusers and say 'No'.

Bullying Children have to learn how to defend their rights against other aggressive children. For some children bullying is a nightmare. If this is happening to your child then you are probably beside yourself with worry and frustration. If the problem is serious, then perhaps involve your child's teacher. Training and encouraging children to be assertive is another way of helping them to cope. If you decide to try to encourage your child to deal with a bully, here are some guidelines that apply equally to other situations where children are the victims of aggressive behaviour.

Building self-esteem
1. Start by building a child's confidence, in much the same way you started to build your own in Chapter One.

2. Talk about the things you like about his or her behaviour, e.g. she is helpful, loves animals etc. Look back at Chapter One and see how you discovered things about yourself and gave yourself a compliment (pages 22–3). Use the same techniques to help the child to find some of the good things which make him likeable and lovable.

3. Help him to understand his rights. Let him add his own.

● The right to be fat

● The right to wear glasses

● The right to read books

● The right not to like sport

● The right _____

● The right _____

● The right _____

4. Help him to understand that he *can* do something about aggressive bullies. (If physical abuse is being used, think about involving teachers.)

5. Encourage him to talk about it:
When does it happen?
What is his usual reaction?
How does he feel?
How would he like to act?

Role play
Role play may be just the thing to help with the problem. By playing the part of the bully, and experimenting with changing his or her behaviour, a child may begin to see how by reacting differently (not always running away to cry or hiding in the toilets) he has some power which he can use against the bully. Standing up to a bully often makes the bully back off, and if it doesn't, it could still make the child feel better to have behaved in a new way.

Other advice
Enlist help and support for the child from other members of the family. Encourage him to act assertively within the family. Ask his opinion about things. Listen to what he has to say. Often a child who is being bullied will completely lose his confidence. Encouraging and supporting him in some of these other areas, where it's easier, can help to restore this confidence.

Just as there's every reason to encourage children, so too older members of the family can benefit from changing their behaviour.

Old dogs learning new tricks
For older people who have always done things one way, any changes can be upsetting and can result in conflict with the rest of the family. It's easy to say, 'We didn't do things that way in my day', but the reality is that today's values are completely different from ones of previous years.

Being old doesn't mean being set in concrete. Older people respond to change just as easily as anyone else. Change is a part of life.

One of the advantages of getting older is that you become wiser and have the hindsight of experience. Combine this wisdom with assertive behaviour to express your feelings – it can transform your family relationships.

Assertiveness and friends

Good friendships are based on equality and respect for each other's rights. Relationships with friends are precious. Good friendships can last a lifetime, while others are more fleeting. Friendship means sharing the good times and the bad; when things go wrong, when there's something to celebrate, when we need reassurance or advice.

The difference between our families and our friends is that we *choose* our friends. Nevertheless good friends often end up being as close as our families, and many of the issues which we have discussed in relation to the family apply to friends.

Involve your friends

Remember that being assertive may mean changing your behaviour. Your close friends will be amongst the first to notice these changes. If you have always gone along passively with what other people think and want, there may be one or two raised eyebrows. If you involve your friends in your efforts to become more assertive, they won't feel excluded. One of the ways you might do this is by asking them to help you with role play exercises. Having honest feed-back from someone you can trust is invaluable.

Change

Like all relationships, friendships change; other people influence them, circumstances alter, a friend may begin to make excessive demands, other difficulties can arise. Being assertive may not put things back to where they were before, but it will allow you to 'clear the air'.

Being assertive in sexual relationships

When the relationship is a sexual one, the issues are even more complex. Relationships in the 1990s involve far more decisions and dilemmas for individuals than in previous decades. Assertiveness cannot resolve all these problems, but it can help to define the limits of a relationship, and the needs of the individuals involved. This may mean an individual's ability to discuss 'safe sex' or ending a relationship. Apart from difficult situations, it can also improve relationships by encouraging partners to express freely their positive feelings about pleasurable sexual activity.

What do I want?

Being assertive in a sexual relationship requires the same self-knowledge as other situations. You have to ask yourself 'What do I feel, and what do I want to happen?'

It's important to learn how to say 'No' to sexual activity which you don't want, and to be able to ask clearly for what you do want. Don't let yourself be manipulated or bullied. Keep asking yourself what *you* want.

Honesty

In relationships which are special, we owe it to each other to be honest. Caring about people and loving them, means we should feel free to behave in an open and honest manner.

The compassion trap

Don't be caught in the compassion trap of thinking that your needs are less important than your partner's, and going along with what they want. Men and women both fall into this trap, for example, making love when they aren't in the mood. In an assertive relationship it becomes natural to say what you feel and what you want, and in turn your partner knows that you understand what they are feeling too. Your needs are equal to your partner's needs. You have the right to say 'I'm not in the mood now'. In the same way your partner has the right to tell you the same thing.

Communicating what we want

Sex is fraught with the possibility of all kinds of misunderstandings. If you mean 'No', make sure that you are sending out that message with your voice and your body. If you want someone to do something – for example, wear a condom – tell him beforehand so that there is no confusion.

Choosing words

Finding the right sexual vocabulary can sometimes make us feel awkward (look back at Chapter One, pages 27–8, on choosing words and the importance of using precise ones). Use simple and straightforward words, and try to find the right time to say them. Make sure that your partner is actually listening to you. Waiting until you are actually in bed is probably a bit too late. Remember that people often feel most vulnerable once they have their clothes off!

My rights

Remember that you have rights in your sexual relationships just as much as in other spheres of your life:

● I have the right to be a sexual person.

● I have the right to enjoy sexual pleasure.

● I have the right to decide with whom I have relationships.

● I have the right to say 'No'.

● I have the right to change my mind.

● I have the right to ask for what I want sexually.

● I have the right to choose my own sexuality.

● I have the right _____

● I have the right _____

● I have the right _____

● I have the right _____

Your Personal Action Plan

Think about this chapter. What was the most important thing you learned? Write it down.

_____

_____

_____

_____

_____

Start and stop

Think of a specific situation which you could improve by *starting* to behave in a different way. Then think of a situation you could improve by *stopping* a particular type of behaviour. The examples can be as simple as you like. The main thing is to choose things which you will be able to achieve, because success with small problems will build your confidence to take on bigger ones. For example, 'I'm going to *stop* screaming at the children because they ignore me anyway, and I'm going to *start* telling them quietly how I feel and asking them to help me with one job – feeding the cats, making their beds, laying the table'.

On the opposite page there is an Action Plan for you to fill in. Be specific. Write down things which you know you can achieve. Write as many things as you want to; there's enough space for you to come back later to add more.

Start simply. Remember you are not trying to change the world yet. There are still more chapters to go!

•

Assertiveness builds positive relationships

•

Action Plan

I am going to start _____

_____

_____

_____

_____

_____

_____

_____

_____

_____

I am going to stop _____

_____

_____

_____

_____

_____

_____

_____

_____

_____

_____

_____

Date _____

CHAPTER THREE

Assertiveness at Work

OBJECTIVES

To help you to:

- handle work relationships
- improve your image at work
- be clear about your objectives
- handle conflicts
- give and take criticism
- negotiate and manage change
- achieve what you want and further your career

SUMMARY

Relationships at work
Behaviour at work: aggressive, passive or assertive?
Criticism
Your profile at work
Communicating
Your annual report to yourself
Power
Working out joint solutions
Pro-active not re-active
Redundancy and employment
Your personal action plan

Relationships at work

Relationships at work are different from other relationships, because they are in the public domain and are contractual arrangements based on money. They are frequently complex: professional; personal; business-like.

They are very often a mixture of the formal and the informal: reprimanding a colleague who is also a friend, or having a social drink after work with the boss. Combining these relationships is quite an art, and being assertive is a key element in mastering that art.

Assertiveness at work – why should it matter?

If you are serious about getting a job, keeping it and perhaps getting promoted, then how you are perceived in the organisation both by your colleagues and by your boss matters. Acting assertively, whether at the interview or in the workplace, can give you a head start on other people.

Handling other people at work Whether you are the giver or receiver of orders, assertiveness – or the lack of it – can make a difference.

Handling an aggressive boss/colleague Taking assertive action can save your sanity. One of my worst experiences was working for a television producer who had suffered a nervous breakdown. As part of his rehabilitation he had been transferred to our department, and I found myself working for a man who was intent on driving the whole team to the very edge. Individual producers, researchers and secretaries were quietly picked off and harassed, some to the point of illness. All of us suffered unnecessary stress, but it was the most assertive and confident members of the team who were least affected by the experience.

Being a passive boss brings problems On one of my courses a participant described the agony he went through with an assistant who wanted the job he got. After he was appointed the assistant went to enormous trouble to undermine him with his superior and the secretarial staff, while being 'utterly supportive' to his face. His life was hell for over a year. It was only after he had moved on that he saw clearly how jealousy had made the assistant behave in such an aggressive and manipulative way. If only he had known how to act more assertively and discussed the situation with all his staff at the time, life would have been a lot easier for him, his family and his colleagues.

Dealing with difficult colleagues like this means relying on your personal resources. You need to feel good about yourself and not allow anyone to undermine you or put excessive pressure on you.

Being responsible for others Assertiveness helps those who have responsibility for others to set realistic limits, to prioritise and to delegate. Clear decision-making gives employees confidence. If people know where they are with a boss, they respond by becoming more assertive themselves and feel confident to express their feelings openly. The result is better team work, better morale all round and in the long run less staff turnover.

Sorting out staff problems Assertiveness also helps to sort out problems of staff behaviour, anything from troublemakers and handling people who aren't pulling their weight to dealing with late-comers and absenteeism.

Decisions about your future prospects Personal behaviour and relationships with colleagues can have a significant impact on decisions made about promotion and redundancy. In a climate of recession being assertive at work is a positive way to behave.

Assertiveness improves job satisfaction

Over the last twenty years my experience of working in a variety of jobs, including local government, waitressing, television production and running my own company, has taught me that the happiest and most productive workplaces are the ones where people are valued as individuals; individuals with rights, able to make occasional mistakes, confident to ask for help and encouraged to speak their minds. The people who run these happy ships are usually confident, assertive types who know what they want – and are respected for it. In almost all cases productivity is high and job satisfaction increases.

Behaviour at work: aggressive, passive or assertive?

Many people behave in a very different way at work. Things which would be normal to say or do at home would be unthinkable in the workplace. The tolerance thresholds of the family are not the same as those of work colleagues. Shouting at your children is one thing, but shouting at your boss is quite another. Understanding how some behaviour is only suited to certain situations is a part of knowing how to show your feelings in an appropriate and positive way.

Your behaviour

There are many reasons why people's behaviour at work differs from that in other places. It is affected by a whole range of things including confidence in their ability to do the work and how well they get on with their colleagues. There are also other factors, such as working under extreme pressure and length of time in the job. Learning to behave in an assertive way at work is no different from behaving in an assertive way with your family and friends. It may require a different approach, but the ground rules are the same. You must know what you feel about a situation, understand the other person's point of view, and have the courage to say what you want in a reasonable way.

Returning to work

For anyone returning to work, anxiety about his or her ability to do the job, can make him feel timid or unsure. Many women tend to show this kind of passive behaviour, and it does nothing to reassure colleagues that they are capable.

It's not unusual to find young men who are equally unsure approaching work in a very different way. They adopt a 'macho' air in order to prove their ability – in the process frequently upsetting colleagues with their aggressive and arrogant behaviour.

Showing feelings

In a work environment it can be difficult to express feelings. Unlike other relationships where speaking your mind is natural, feelings about people's behaviour are frequently left unexpressed. The result is a festering mass of resentment and anger, with individuals feeling under-valued and used, or resorting to outbursts of uncontrolled rage. Saying what you feel and what you want is as important at work as it is in other spheres of life.

Put-downs

These remarks are designed to make you feel small or to manipulate you into doing something which you don't want to say or do. Put-downs at work are common. Some are delivered quite blatantly, but others are subtly disguised in jokey behaviour which is difficult to confront.

For example: 'The trouble with you is you've no sense of humour. Why do you take everything so seriously?'

Put-downs are a way of trying to negate your rights. Dealing assertively with them doesn't necessarily mean giving the quick and cutting response (much as we would all love to be able to do this!). Often it is better merely to recognise it as aggressive behaviour. But let the other person know that you understand the hidden *aggressive* message and that you don't like this kind of behaviour.

Dealing with put-downs
Try the 'Drip Method' which is taken from the Broken Record technique of repeating your message, described in Chapter One (see page 41).

1. Deny what is said.

2. Say something good about yourself.

3. Make it clear you dislike the person's behaviour.

4. Repeat your message as many times as necessary.

5. Repeat it the next time the put-down is used.

For example: 'I have a perfectly good sense of humour. Your behaviour isn't funny'.

By doing this you feel more relaxed and confident because you know that this will be your response in a similar situation in the future. Try thinking of any common put-downs which you may experience, such as 'That's a typical woman's response'. Write down a good 'Drip Method' response, for example, 'It's my reaction and it feels right to me'.

The put-down _____

_____

The response _____

_____

The put-down _____

_____

_____

The response _____

_____

_____

Criticism

During our working life most of us will be on the giving and receiving ends of criticism, and it's important to distinguish what is valid and what is invalid criticism.

Learning to deal with it assertively is important: *negative criticism* can undermine self-confidence but *constructive criticism* helps to boost self-confidence.

Receiving criticism

Criticism at work is so often given as a put-down or in an aggressive manner that the receiver feels on the defensive from the start. Being criticised is a source of anxiety and tension to some people and like 'a red rag to a bull' to others. How do you deal with criticism? There are three things to consider:

● The criticism

● The behaviour of the giver

● Your reaction.

The criticism
1. Listen carefully to what is said. Is there any truth in it?

2. Make sure you understand why it's being given.

3. If you don't understand, ask for clarification. For example, to a generalised criticism like 'You really aren't pulling your weight', ask, 'could you give me an example?'

4. Take time to decide on the truth of what is being said. Check: (a) Is it completely true?
 (b) Is it partly true?
 (c) Is it untrue?

5. If in doubt ask other people if they agree.

6. Decide to change your behaviour if it's useful.

The behaviour of the giver

1. Is it being given aggressively or assertively?

2. How do you feel about the way it is being given, and what is your reaction to the person's behaviour?

Action: Decide to respond assertively to the criticism.

If it is true:	You could say:
Agree with it –	'Yes, I forgot to send both letters.'
Explain how you feel –	'I feel upset about it.'
Ask why it matters –	'Will it make things difficult?'
If it is partly true:	
Agree with the bit that is partly true –	'I did forget to send one letter.'
Say how you feel –	'I feel disappointed that you think that of me.'
Make clear that the rest is untrue –	'All the other mail went. It was an oversight.'
When it's untrue:	
Reject the criticism –	'I sent all the mail.'
Add your positive thoughts –	'I am a very responsible and reliable member of staff.'
Ask for an explanation –	'Why did you think that I hadn't sent it?'

Using criticism constructively:

1. Deal with it.

2. Decide what you can learn from the experience.

3. Decide on changes to your behaviour.

4. Then put it out of your mind – you have dealt with it and no useful purpose is served by going over and over it as you lie in bed at night.

Giving criticism

Criticism should be constructive. It should be used to put things right, to encourage people to behave differently and to boost workers' confidence in their abilities. Good criticism is an assertive way of bringing about change.

1. Know what you want to say and why.

2. Which specific behaviour are you criticising?

3. Choose the right time and place.

4. Use specific words and avoid vague generalisations.

5. Comment on behaviour and not on the person.

6. Say how you feel.

7. Say what changes you'd like to see.

8. Acknowledge that the person has the right to accept or reject the criticism.

9. Express your willingness to discuss the issue and work out a joint solution.

10. State what you have agreed.

Difficult people

Being able to give criticism assertively makes it easier to deal with difficult people. Whether receiving or giving criticism, assertiveness helps people to communicate what they feel. Think about a difficult situation at work where someone else's behaviour is affecting you. For example, I remember one job where I worked for a sarcastic (aggressive) workaholic. I still recall vividly how I reacted to his behaviour. I would have written:

'I work as a local government officer. Every day I feel sick as I drive to work. Peter behaves as though I have done something wrong. He looks at his watch the minute I arrive, even when I'm early. I feel guilty, so I behave as though I've done something wrong and scurry to my desk hoping he'll stop looking at me. I'd like to walk in with my head held high, look at my watch and say "Good morning" in a cheery voice.'

Can you describe a similar situation?

I work as _____

_____

_____

Describe the situation _____

_____

_____

_____

Describe the person's behaviour _____

_____

_____

_____

_____

Describe how you feel _____

_____

_____

_____

_____

Describe your behaviour _____

_____

_____

_____

_____

Describe what you would like to do _____

_____

_____

_____

_____

All workplaces have their share of problems. With so many competing personalities and egos jockeying for position, it can all seem a bit much at times. People get locked into situations which are almost unresolvable. Being assertive in these difficult situations probably won't solve the problem but it is one positive way forward when things seem very bleak.

Exercise: Imagine you are working for a large organisation where a new man has been brought in, a man promoted beyond his ability. He takes a dislike to you, blames you for everything that goes wrong. You suspect he wants to get rid of you. Jobs are hard to find. Listed on the opposite page are various things you can do.

Look at the options. How would you describe the different behaviours? Tick the appropriate box?

a. Have a blazing row and leave.

b. Ask to be transferred to a smaller, regional office.

c. Do nothing, feel unhappy, grumble and spread rumours.

d. Speak to your personnel officer, ask for help and try to work towards improving things.

e. Decide you can't stay. Use the time to look for another job and leave when you're ready to leave.

f. Talk to the man and try to resolve the problem?

	AGGRESSIVE	ASSERTIVE	PASSIVE
Do you think that a is			
Do you think that b is			
Do you think that c is			
Do you think that d is			
Do you think that e is			
Do you think that f is			

Key: See page 142 for answers.

Your profile at work

The way you are regarded at work will have quite a lot to do with the way you behave towards your colleagues. They will have formed an impression of you, which you will reinforce every day by the way you do or don't respond to events. There are five things to think about:

1. How you see yourself.
2. How others see you.
3. How you feel.
4. How you act.
5. How you communicate.

How you see yourself

Look at the following chart and choose which description describes the way you think that you usually act at work. Remember, your behaviour at work may be very different from your behaviour in other places and with other people.

AGGRESSIVE	PASSIVE	ASSERTIVE
I know what I want and I usually get it.	I prefer to keep quiet. I don't like to be outspoken.	I like being involved in what's going on.
My career is vital. I want promotion It's kill or be killed.	If I don't rock the boat I should be OK for the rest of my working life.	I work to live, not live to work.
Other people know what I'm like and have to put up with me.	I don't always know what I want, so usually I let others decide.	I work out what I want, listen to others and then discuss the plans.
I don't suffer fools gladly. I like to win.	I'd rather not cause a fuss, but I feel that people ignore me.	I like people to know how I feel.

By now you should be beginning to have an idea of the kind of behaviour you use at work. Write down any other phrase which particularly describes your behaviour, for example 'I like to be unpredictable and keep people on their toes'.

_____

_____

_____

_____

_____

How others see you

Work involves routine and certain expectations of patterns of behaviour. Our colleagues form their impression of us from this behaviour, and it is in this way that our 'reputation', for better or worse, is established. Changing this impression requires positive action.

Assertive action

There are various ways we can improve the impression we give. Most of them don't require huge changes, just an awareness of how we behave now, and if we think it could improve, then making a decision to do something positive.

Acting more decisively Use assertiveness techniques to make up your mind. Colleagues are impressed when we are clear about what we feel and what we want to happen. They may not always agree with us, but at least they know where we stand on issues, and this gains their respect.

Image We can all improve our image relatively easily. At work, the rewards for employees with a good image are high: promotion, responsibility, involvement in decisions, respect and so on. Apart from our ability to do the job, our image is the most influential factor in how we are regarded. Behaviour, appearance, body language and confidence all contribute to the image which we present in the office.

What kind of an image have you got? Are you serious, reliable, a workaholic, the office joker, a bit of a dog's body, or a time-waster?

Write down what you think your present image is ____ ____

_____

_____

_____

Write down what image you would like to have _____

_____

_____

_____

_____

Body language In Chapter One we discussed the importance of body language in reinforcing our words. Look at page 34.

In the office, body language is just as important and can be used in different ways. For example, if you're trying to reach a joint solution, sitting behind a desk in a manner which says 'I'm the boss' may not make the other person feel free to express his or her views. Standing directly in front of people, or over them, can be threatening, especially if they feel their space is being invaded. Being too far away has the opposite effect, it makes the person feel alienated. Your body language should reassure the person that you are both working together on the issue. Try experimenting and see the difference it can make.

Confidence: playing the part I remember how nervous I felt when I got my first job in a chemist's shop in Blackpool. I was 15 and still at school. Once I had got the job I was terrified. I had never served in a shop before. How would I cope with customers? How was I going to do it? They would find out I was just a schoolgirl. I felt really sick with worry. I decided that I would pretend. Every day before I went to work I would put on my overall and imagine I was a 'real' shop assistant getting ready for work. The result was that I found I had become a shop assistant and my confidence grew. It was such a good idea that I've always used it. I think of it as 'Playing the Part' or 'Putting on my Costume' for whatever the occasion is. But it's more than that. It is a way of building your self-confidence by using your imagination and accepting that you are very capable of taking on all sorts of new responsibilities. It has continued to help me in all kinds of situations; from jobs where I didn't have experience, like waitressing, to ones where I had the experience but hadn't had authority before, as a new film director with a very aggressive, woman-hating cameraman.

Dressing the part Wearing the right clothes boosts self-confidence and lends authority to your presence. It also reinforces your ability to act assertively and is a very good technique to adopt. If you are feeling very run down and weary *do not* go into work wearing your old suit and a grease-spotted tie. Dressing in an assertive and confident way will help you to feel better.

In combination with body language, dressing the part can influence your state of mind. It won't necessarily take away a problem, but it is a practical way of demonstrating that you have control over one important thing – your appearance and your image.

Communicating

People who don't communicate at work drive everyone else mad and cause enormous problems. Relying on telepathy is no use. Good communication relies on being clear what you want in a situation and making sure that your message is understood by the other person. If you don't communicate well, the chances are that you will have unsatisfactory relationships with other employees.

Remember:

● Tell people what you feel and think.

● Tell people what you want.

● Listen to what they have to say.

● Re-state your case.

● Look for joint agreement.

Scoring own goals

It is very easy to give a false impression. You can be your own worst enemy. Using phrases like, 'Oh, I'm so forgetful I can never remember anything' or, 'I just can't organise anything in my life' are prime examples of scoring own goals. People won't disagree. They will just use your words to confirm their negative impression of you. We often use phrases which could give the wrong impression of our abilities. Listen to yourself, and write down any you use, similar to the ones above. If you can't think of any now, don't worry, just listen to yourself over the next few days.

_____

_____

_____

Look at what you have written.
What impression do these words give?
Is it an impression which will impress colleagues?

Avoid saying negative things They confirm other people's prejudices and reinforce feelings of hopelessness. Stressing negative points is not the way to impress colleagues.

Look for positive things Boost your self-confidence by taking some time to write a list of things you know you do well at work. There are different things you can consider – your personal skills, your technical or professional ability, your physical stamina – anything which *you* know you do well and in which you take a pride. It could be something quite small which gives you a real feeling of satisfaction. Write down what's important to you, and on days when you feel low, take this list out and look at it. For example, I might write: 'I have a good telephone manner', 'I can fold napkins perfectly', 'I have taught myself to use a word processor very efficiently', 'I have run some excellent and enjoyable workshops', 'I have the stamina to carry heavy filming equipment'. *Write as many as you like.*

Personal skills _____

_____

_____

_____

Technical/Professional skills _____

_____

_____

_____

Physical skills _____

_____

_____

_____

Your annual report to yourself

Many organisations and companies now have annual reports and appraisals of their staff. This is an opportunity for employees to look at their performance during the year and, with the help of their personnel officer and boss, to assess their progress and development within the company.

Your assertiveness appraisal

Giving ourselves an annual appraisal on personal behaviour and performance is an extension of this idea.

The report On the opposite page there is an Annual Report for you to write. It is an opportunity to examine how your behaviour affects other people and how that in turn affects the working atmosphere – good things as well as not so good. It will help you to identify problems, and will give you confidence to know that you are already behaving well in some areas of your working life.

Think about the answers, particularly those where behaviour is a part of the problem. Would behaving differently help to resolve a situation?

Targets

Identify what you intend to target for action. Perhaps adopting more assertive behaviour in certain situations, for example, 'I'm going to speak up and say what I feel at meetings' or, 'I'm going to tell the office groper to stop touching me every time he passes my desk'. Decide on action for the next six months. Just write it down for the moment. You don't have to *do* anything yet. This will be a useful record. Come back to it in six months and see what has changed.

●

Assertiveness works for you

●

Your Annual Assertiveness Appraisal

Your name: *Your job description:*

Date:

Your general behaviour (give examples of your recent assertive, aggressive or passive behaviour)

_____

_____

_____

_____

Your relationships: superiors, subordinates and colleagues

_____

_____

_____

_____

Difficult situations which may have arisen

_____

_____

_____

_____

_____

Your behaviour in that situation

_____

_____

_____

_____

Difficult relationships (say with whom and why)

_____

_____

_____

_____

_____

Your behaviour in that relationship

_____

_____

_____

_____

_____

Good relationships (say with whom and why)

_____

_____

_____

_____

_____

Your behaviour in that relationship

_____

_____

_____

_____

_____

Your strengths at work (make sure these are strengths, don't mistake being a door mat with loyalty)

_____

_____

_____

_____

Areas for improvement, e.g. saying what I think

_____

_____

_____

_____

Targets (identify specific things and set a date)

_____

_____

_____

Power

Power should not be confused with authority. Authority may come with a job, but power has to be developed. Look at people with authority in your workplace. Different managers with similar authority will all have varying levels of power, according to the way they have used and developed it.

Power is a two-way process which involves relationships. Understanding the different types of power, and how they are used, is important in establishing equality in those relationships. Most of us don't stop to think about our power at work, we see it as 'He's the boss, I'm the employee', when in fact there are many different types of power which we can all use: Everyone has some power, regardless of his or her position. It may not be power over others but power in relation to the organisation. The man who controls the car parking spaces wields enormous power, so too does the telephone receptionist who puts you 'on hold'.

Power comes in various forms:

- the power (authority) over other employees
- the power which comes from specific skills, for example being the only German-speaker
- the power of a professional qualification which sets an employee apart, for example the company doctor
- the power of communication and interpersonal skills.

Power nets

Organisations have both a power structure and a hierarchy. The two are not necessarily the same. I have known organisations where the man who controlled the office supplies seemed to have far more power than the office manager. In some companies the ladies on the tea bar have enormous power – tea ladies often know who's up to what. Some of the most influential (powerful) people I have worked with have not been at the top, they have been people who did their jobs efficiently and effectively and in the process gained the respect of everyone and built themselves a power net. Aggressive people sometimes build power nets based on fear. Passive people usually fail abysmally. Assertive people's power nets are strong and flexible.

Identify different types of power Begin to identify how colleagues use their authority, their power and their influence.

Identify your personal power Regardless of your position within the hierarchy – managing director, receptionist or tea boy – you have personal power to control your own behaviour and to influence others. Assertiveness means being aware of personal power and using it well. Having identified different kinds of power in others think about your own.

● What kind of power do you have?

● Do you have authority over people or things?

● What personal skills or special qualifications do you have?

● What resources do you control?

● Are there any areas of power you could develop?

Think about your power and see how you can make it work positively *with* the power of others. Working out your position in power terms, in relation to colleagues, can make you feel more confident about your position within an organisation. It also tells you where the real power lies.

Exercise: Think of two people you work closely with. Include those above and below you. What sort of a power relationship exists between you? What kind of power, authority or influence do they have over you, and what is it based on? How do they use it? For example, an accountant's power over the money you spend, or your secretary's power over your diary. I've included my own example on the next page.

For example: Name: Jane. Position: Office manager. Power: Authority and influence. Based on: Her position in the organisation and her knowledge and experience. How it's used: Uses both well. Treats me like an equal.

Now complete your own power net.

My Power Net **Their** *Power in relation to* **me**

Name _____

Power _____

_____

_____

Based on _____

_____

_____

How it's used _____

_____

_____

Name _____

Power _____

_____

_____

Based on _____

_____

_____

How it's used _____

_____

_____

Using the same list ask what kind of power, authority or influence **you** *have in relation to* **them**.

My Power Net *My Power in relation to* **them**
For example, Name: Jane. My Power: Influence. Based on: My experience and reputation. How I use it: To negotiate approval for recruiting new staff and starting new projects

Name _____

My power _____

_____

Based on _____

_____

_____

How I use it _____

_____

_____

Name _____

My power _____

_____

Based on _____

_____

_____

How I use it _____

_____

Identifying our wider work power net can be a useful exercise. Remember, power is a two-way relationship and you are part of that relationship. You are not as 'powerless' as you might imagine. Another constructive exercise is to imagine yourself as being at the centre of a spider's web. Think of all your colleagues as being around you in the web and draw power lines between you and them. Later you can see how your colleagues relate to each other by drawing lines across the web. It's interesting to see how people's webs of power intertwine and it can give you a better insight into relationships in your workplace.

The balance of power

Understanding power gives us confidence to tackle problems at work, which are often caused by *misuse* of power. If we don't act assertively and exert *our* power in these situations, we are colluding with the perpetrators and adding to the problem. Pretending there's nothing wrong, while bottling up feelings of resentment or of being persecuted, will do nothing for your self-esteem, let alone resolve the conflict.

Misuse of power All workplaces have their share of problem people who misuse their power or behave badly – jokers, time wasters, gossips, workaholics, alcoholics and even the boss. Dealing with them isn't easy. Being on the receiving end of someone's sarcasm or put-downs can be very demoralising.

A problem raised on a recent course was the difficulty a young graphic designer had trying to cope with a foul-mouthed boss who was forever making offensive sexual remarks. She wanted to keep her job, which she loved, but the strain of working with such an insensitive person was really intolerable. The reality is that she is one of thousands of people who suffer similar offensive behaviour. Being assertive is one way of trying to cope with these very difficult situations.

Tackling the mis-use of power Problems with bullies, liars, trouble makers, sexual harassers or wimps have one thing in common – behaviour. If you start by concentrating on the behaviour and not on the person, this allows a certain amount of emotional detachment, which is important.

If someone at work continually puts you down in front of people, leaving you feeling embarrassed, confused and angry, start by examining the problem away from the office. This allows you time and space to think about the situation on your own territory. This could help to make you feel a bit more secure.

Look at the behaviour:

1. Is it aggressive or passive?

2. What is the purpose of the behaviour?

3. Ask yourself what you feel. Express this clearly.

4. Try to relax and work out what you want to happen.

As yet you have only identified the behaviour. There is no need to take any action. Wait until you feel strong and confident. If you act before you are ready, another put-down will make you feel worse.

Behaviour and power

Think about the power the person with the behaviour problem has, and think about your power in relation to that person. Decide what action is appropriate under the circumstances. Realising that power is a two-way process should give you more confidence to assert your rights.

Choose the right moment to use your assertiveness skills. Confronting someone just as he begins is a good moment, and can stop him in his tracks.

In the case of the young graphic designer, it was suggested that the next time her boss starts his sexual innuendos, she might say, 'I find your behaviour is very offensive and I would prefer it if you didn't speak about me like that again' This could be difficult because he could of course take powerful action, and fire her. However, she has power too: the power of her talent and good work; her good relationships with other members of the team; the respect of the clients whose accounts she handles. So he might think twice about acting rashly.

The sexist and racist factor

Sexist and racist behaviour is still rampant in workplaces and makes life very difficult and unequal for many women and minority groups. Although more organisations are introducing equal opportunities policies, age-old chauvinistic behaviour doesn't disappear overnight. Behaving assertively, whether you are a man or a woman, helps to create an environment where equal opportunities exist for all the workforce.

Experiencing sexist 'put-downs', being asked (illegal) interview questions about coping with children, being the butt of racist jokes, are all commonplace. Individuals learn to deal with them in their own ways, mainly by being passive, letting it go, or saying nothing. Using assertive behaviour, similar to the technique for put-downs described on pages 84–5, can bring results. Say quite firmly that you do not like the behaviour. Even if the perpetrator's response is aggressive (which it probably will be), keep calm and don't launch into a vitriolic counter-attack (aggressive). Standing firm can eventually change things, and meanwhile you have the satisfaction of having said something positive.

In the case of a sexist or racist question at an interview, you are within your rights to say firmly that the question is out of order, and it is illegal to ask it. I heard of an 18-year-old female student who recently applied to medical school. She was asked by an eminent professor at the interview if she intended to take contraceptive precautions! More recently a woman colleague applying for a senior television post was asked at the board how she would look after her two children! Sexism dies hard.

Supporting colleagues It may be a colleague who's on the end of the offensive remarks. Speaking up and saying, 'I don't like what I heard' takes courage. Supporting colleagues in this way calls for strong assertive action, which will increase your own feelings of self-worth.

Go slowly Confronting an office bully, someone who is sexually harassing you, a work mate who is behaving badly, or a racist employer, takes courage and, like all the other things about learning to be assertive, it takes time. Practice on some less difficult things which are achievable and which will boost your confidence.

Less serious issues

If the situation is more practical, perhaps whether the office should be a no-smoking area, then it may be easier to raise it without being threatened by power.

In all cases listen to what other people want to say about their feelings. This doesn't mean agreeing with them, but does mean that they know they have been heard. Repeat your needs and, if it's appropriate, indicate that there is room for negotiation to work out a joint solution.

In the case of the offensive boss there is less, if any, room for compromise, but in the case of the no-smoking office it's easier to think of possible solutions.

Working out joint solutions

Work relationships are no different from other relationships when it comes to using assertiveness skills to work out joint agreements.

1. State your position. How you feel in the circumstances and what outcome you want.

2. Acknowledge your colleague's feelings. For example, 'I can see that you are angry. What is the matter?' (When dealing with any strong feelings it's important to react calmly and to give reassurance that you are hearing what is being said.) This doesn't mean agreeing with them, merely demonstrating an understanding of the other person's position.

3. Continually ask yourself what you feel and if it's fair.

4. Say if you believe it is unfair, and explain why.

5. State clearly and firmly what *you* want.

6. Be constructive in your comments.

7. Communicate clearly, and look for joint compromise.

When dealing with aggressive behaviour remember that people are frequently aggressive at work in order to hide their feelings of insecurity or incompetence. They use bad-tempered and ill-mannered behaviour as a way of pretending that they're in control, when the reverse is often the case. Understanding this may help to distance the person and keep emotions at bay. It may not be much consolation when you are on the receiving end of a fiery blast from someone, or are being cold-shouldered, but remember this is a technique of self-protection, which can be helpful.

Exercise: Look back to page 89 where you wrote down an example of a difficult situation at work where someone's behaviour was affecting you. Using that same example look at the behaviour of the other person, ask how you feel about the behaviour and what you want to happen. For example, I would write: 'Peter is behaving in a manipulative and aggressive way. I feel angry that I allow myself to respond to his clock-watching tactics by feeling guilty. I want to discuss the situation with him, tell him how I feel about his behaviour, and make sure he is clear about the hours I work and the commitment I have.'

Using the example on page 89 describe the other person's behaviour.
He/she is behaving _____

_____

_____

_____

_____

I feel _____

_____

_____

_____

I want to _____

_____

_____

_____

Role play

Perhaps just re-reading this situation makes you feel nervous, sick or worried inside. Many people feel just like this. One way of trying to deal with it is to use role play which is described on page 37 in Chapter One. Try taking the example you have written about above, and use it in a role play session with your partner. (Read the guidelines for role play and feedback before attempting this.)

If the problem is with your boss, brief your partner about the situation and act out the scene. For example, you could play yourself reacting to another request to stay late. Your partner would play the boss listening to you stating your case. Ask him/her to react as the boss might react. Continue to be assertive throughout – calm, cool and rational even under provocation.

See what happens, and then ask your partner for feedback. Then try changing roles.

Role playing and feedback are helpful in seeing problems at work in a different light. Looking at work situations from another perspective gives an understanding of the other person's problems. If helps to clarify what action to take and where there might be areas of joint agreement.

Understanding other people's feelings and needs is all part of behaving responsibly and assertively.

Pro-active not re-active

So far we've looked at situations which already exist. Problems which have been allowed to develop over a period of time. One of the big advantages of assertiveness is that when it's used well, it prevents problems arising.

Being pro-active means taking the initiative in situations, not waiting for something to happen before reacting. Assertive people try to take action before the axe falls. That's not to say that they don't have their share of work problems, but being assertive improves the way they are regarded by colleagues, which in turn improves their status in the eyes of most bosses. Assertive people tend to be involved and know what's going on.

Being assertive helps if the worst happens, and if it doesn't, then you are contributing to a better work environment.

During my working life I've been unemployed, made redundant and passed over for promotion, none of them experiences which I would particularly like to go through again. As I grew more assertive, each experience, although hurtful, did in fact become easier to cope with, because I realised that I was still the same person inside. I hadn't changed, only the circumstances had. I had exactly the same rights as I had had before. In this way, being assertive helped me to pick myself up and move on to even more rewarding experiences.

Redundancy and unemployment

The possibility of redundancy and unemployment tends to concentrate the mind amazingly quickly. Sometimes there are warning signs that trouble is brewing and immediate action is called for. At other times it comes out of the blue. Some years ago I was training redundant male executives on a fairly regular basis. Before the experience of being made redundant they had never thought about their behaviour. Once they were in the world of the unemployed, however, they were anxious to learn fast. Teaching assertiveness skills to such receptive people was very rewarding. They responded enthusiastically to something they could see would positively enhance their chances of finding new work and keeping it.

Interviews for new jobs

If the worst happens and you do become unemployed then think about how to use your assertiveness in your search for new work and particularly in the interviews you will get. There are many pieces of research which show that self-presentation is far more important than knowledge itself when it comes to getting a job.

Tips for presenting yourself

In an interview you will feel tense and under pressure. Use your assertiveness skills – remember the breathing techniques, relax, speak clearly, listen to the other side and try to relate to the interviewers and their questions.

● Prepare yourself. Re-read pages 94 and 95 on playing the part. If wearing a smart suit makes you feel uncomfortable, remind yourself that this is all part of the performance.

● Enter the interview room in an assured way. Try to maintain a relaxed and confident air. Look again at the section in Chapter One on body language.

● Greet the interviewers with a warm smile.

● Sit comfortably. Don't slouch or hunch up.

● No matter how you feel, try to enjoy it.

● Remember an interview is just another relationship and *you* can make it work to your benefit by appearing outwardly confident (even if you are terrified inside).

● An interview is a two-way process. Being assertive will help you to express yourself and establish a rapport with the interviewers.

Managing change

In any organisation, change is inevitable. Whether it's change at the top, relocation of the company, or being taken over by a multi-national, change can be painful. Behaving in an assertive manner is a way of helping you to cope with difficult and changing situations.

Encouraging others to be assertive

In situations where other colleagues are under extreme pressure, behaving assertively not only lends moral support, but encourages others to act likewise. Joint assertive action is influential. Seeing the glimmer of hope in a bad situation can inspire others to press for change.

Learning from other people

Watching how other people behave, and the effect their behaviour has on others, is one of the best ways we can learn. Identify the successful and respected people in your workplace. Watch how they behave.

Exercise: Think of one individual in your work life who has influenced you, and whose qualities, both as an individual and as a colleague, you admire. It's probably someone who makes work enjoyable and who behaves very assertively.

Write down his or her name _____

His or her qualities as a work colleague _____

_____

_____

_____

Examples of his or her assertive behaviour

_____

_____

_____

Exercise: Your qualities Based on the description above, write down some similar qualities about yourself, your work, relationships and your assertive behaviour which make you a successful and respected colleague. For example: 'I try to keep my office door open for anyone to come in, people ask my advice, people trust me, I make decisions quickly, I'm good at sorting out disagreements etc.' *Make your own list.*

In my work I _____

_____

_____

_____

_____

_____

_____

_____

_____

_____

_____

Your Personal Action Plan

Think about this chapter. What was the most important thing you learned? Write it down.

_____

_____

_____

_____

_____

_____

Start and stop

As in previous chapters this is your chance to make specific decisions about things you intend to start and stop doing. Think of things which would improve your competence, ability and relationships at work.

●

Assertiveness means having
rights and responsibilities

●

Action Plan

I am going to start _____

_____

_____

_____

_____

_____

_____

_____

_____

_____

I am going to stop _____

_____

_____

_____

_____

_____

_____

_____

_____

_____

_____

_____

Date _____

CHAPTER FOUR

Assertiveness in the Community

OBJECTIVES

To help you to:
- be assertive in daily life
- communicate with neighbours
- feel more confident in public
- know what you want and resolve situations
- deal with authorities
- deal with nameless individuals
- cope with unexpected situations

SUMMARY

Being assertive in a wider context
Different relationships in the community
Gaining confidence
Dealing with neighbours
Your rights
Dealing with the community
Official bodies
Dealing with the unexpected
Your personal action plan

Being assertive in a wider context

In previous chapters you have learned how to develop assertive relationships with people you know well – your family,
your friends and your work colleagues. Learning to be assertive in the community where you live, with people whom you
perhaps don't know, is just as important.

In today's society, unless we are prepared to be assertive we
can very easily lose out on our rights and find that decisions
are taken by others which affect us personally and financially: making sure we get the right allowances from social
security; questioning bank charges, and so on. On a more
practical level, being assertive gives us confidence to say
publicly what we want: asking for a seat on a crowded bus
when carrying a baby and the shopping; sorting out a problem with the neighbours and noisy teenagers; ensuring that
local planners take our needs into consideration. Assertiveness can also help us to be more in control, and behave more
confidently, when unpleasant and unexpected things occur,
anything from obscene phone calls to accidents.

Why bother?

Apart from the practical benefits, acting assertively will
clarify the situation for both sides. You may end up better off,
financially or materially, and there's a sense of personal
achievement when you know you've taken firm action. On a
recent course, one man arrived in a state of fury. He recently
challenged a parking ticket which had been issued when the
meter failed to work properly. He had written to explain the
circumstances, and that morning had received a letter back
saying that as they had no other complaints about the meter
he would have to pay the fine. It was easy to point out to him
that they were 'fogging' the issue; see page 41. He had every
right to complain. It was suggested that he wrote again and
said that regardless of them not having received other complaints, *he* was complaining that the meter was faulty and he
did not intend to pay the fine. (This is using the 'Broken

Record' technique; see page 41.) I saw him several weeks later and he was delighted to tell me that he had received a second reply saying that under the circumstances the fine would be waived. A successful, assertive experience which left him feeling good, and not out of pocket. Determination is part of being assertive, so don't be put off by the first negative response you get.

Different relationships in the community

Everybody's community is different. Living in a city with thousands of people may be very different from living in a small village with only a handful of people, but whatever the size of the community the relationships within it have many things in common.

Neighbours

We all have neighbours, whether they live in the flat upstairs or some distance down the road. Our relationships with them develop because of living close together, meeting regularly and having common concerns. Keeping good relationships going and improving ones that aren't so good can take a lot of effort. Misunderstandings can arise over the simplest things, so good communication is a must. There's more about this later in the chapter.

The local community

There are people in our community who aren't neighbours, but whom we know quite well – local shopkeepers and business people, our doctor or dentist, our children's teachers. With many of these people we have a more formal relationship, for example with our bank manager or the doctor. We may know their name, but their job or 'position' in the community gives them status. Sometimes this can over-awe us and create an unequal relationship. Assertiveness helps us to feel more equal in these types of relationships and feel more comfortable about saying what we feel.

Official bodies

These are what I call 'faceless organisations': the tax people, social security, the Department of Employment, the Law Courts, local councils, insurance companies and so on. They are impersonal and frequently large off-putting organisations. Experience shows that we need to have determination, patience and a clear idea of what we want, before starting to deal with the people who staff them. There's more later in the chapter about persevering and the results it brings.

Common ground Whether you're dealing with neighbours, restaurant managers, offices, banks or institutions, remind yourself that you are dealing with *people* and that it is possible to develop a good assertive relationship with people. Of course, there will be times when you meet difficult people who refuse to acknowledge you as a person. They may behave in a very dismissive (aggressive) manner, but don't let them put you off. Continue to behave assertively and say what you want to happen. Remember these people are usually the exception.

Finding out their name It's usually easier to deal with people if you know their name. It's more personal. Remember that your new assertive behaviour is all about communicating in a better way with people. If you don't know their name then you start off at a disadvantage.

When dealing with organisations where several people answer the phone or deal with enquiries, always write down the name of the person you are speaking to. Asking for that person next time will save you from being passed around, while people 'look for your file', and then ask you the same questions you were asked on your first enquiry. Establishing a relationship with someone in the organisation means you are already becoming 'an individual' in their eyes.

There are other circumstances, for example where a salesman is being rude and unhelpful, when asking assertively for the person's name may make them improve their behaviour. (They may think you will report them to their boss, but they also know from your attitude that you mean business.) Try it out and see the result for yourself.

Gaining confidence

The rules are the same as those for being assertive in other situations. Ask yourself what you feel and what you want to happen, and find the best way of communicating it. Look back at Chapter One, pages 25–8.

Assertive behaviour will give you confidence to deal with neighbours, estate agents, bankers, undertakers, electricity boards, council officials or anyone in a position of authority. It will strengthen your message and help you to achieve what *you* want.

The difference between dealing with people in the wider community and our friends and families is that we feel more exposed. Gaining confidence in our ability to behave assertively in public takes time and practice. Before we even think about saying anything we have to *feel* confident in our appearance.

Appearing confident

Part of *feeling* confident is knowing that you *appear* confident to other people. We looked at this in relation to work in Chapter Three (see page 94). You could use these ideas in these new situations.

Even people who appear in public regularly will tell you that they frequently feel nervous. Many celebrities who are able to speak to a big audience find it impossible to deal with problems like complaining in a restaurant or taking faulty goods back to a shop. They admit to feeling uncomfortable and sick at the thought of 'making a fool of themselves'. It's reassuring to know that other, so-called 'confident people' feel just the same nervousness that we do.

Conquering nerves and panic

It takes practice and time to conquer nerves and control feelings of panic, but it is possible. The importance of the issue may help. It's a question of weighing up how much something matters to us, compared to those feelings of nervousness or panic. If we have strong feelings about the situation we may feel that we can't keep quiet any longer. At this point the adrenalin takes over and the nerves generally decrease or disappear. Think of a situation where you have 'spoken your mind' to someone. Perhaps in a shop when you were facing a rude assistant, or in a hotel where they had given you a dingy room. How did you behave? How did you appear to others? Was it aggressive, passive or assertive? Write the situation down below and say how you felt.

Sometimes it's easier if you are speaking out on behalf of someone else. For example, I can remember asking for the doctor to visit a relative who had become ill, suddenly. The receptionist was not co-operative. I had to become insistent almost to the point of anger. I used very strong assertive behaviour. Afterwards I felt good, and relieved. The doctor came and the relative was in fact admitted to hospital.

Write down your example below.

The situation _____

_____

What action you took _____

_____

_____

The kind of behaviour _____

How you felt about it _____

_____

_____

Be careful not to appear aggressive Being confident is one thing but if we have strong feelings about something it can easily lead to aggressive behaviour, or be seen as aggressive by others. Remember that being assertive means being aware of other people's rights too.

Developing a confident manner Look back at the section on body language in Chapter One (pages 34–5). Also look at image and how others see us in Chapter Three (pages 91–5). Remember, your body language should reinforce what you are saying.

Opening your mouth in public Some people find this such a nerve-wracking ordeal that their voice disappears or goes squeaky and shrill. Even the thought of complaining about something makes them want to curl up and die. If you feel like this, don't worry; this book is meant only to encourage you to do the things that you want to do, and no more. However, it's worth remembering that you will face situations at some point in life where speaking out is crucial to a decision: which hospital you go into, which school your child goes to, stopping planners from putting a road through your garden and so on. At times like these, you will be grateful that you learned to be assertive.

Using your voice

Go back to the mirror exercise on pages 22–3 and think of some things in your wider community life you would like to change. Say them out loud as you did in Chapter One.

Volume Listen carefully to your voice. Can you make it sound louder without shouting? Remember, if you're going to tell someone what you think about a situation they have to hear what you say. Make sure your voice is clear, and that you can control its volume when you need to. Speaking to your neighbour requires a different approach from dealing with a group of people in a public meeting.

Exercise: Projecting your voice. Stand in your bathroom (or wherever you practise). Try saying the phrase 'I am going to deliver a speech' in four different ways: first as if you are speaking to one person, then to six people, then to sixty people and finally to six hundred.

Notice the difference both in the volume of your voice and in the way you project it.

Choose the right words Again look at Chapter One for some guidance. Choose words which will help you to get your message across. Say what you feel about things. You have the right to put your view forward. Don't be put off by the gobbledygook language of bureaucracies. Use the words which make your message clear.

Tackling issues

Start with simple things. Successfully telling the butcher that the meat you bought last week was tough, could be a major achievement. Each success will increase your confidence. Suddenly you will find that by behaving assertively you can start to put things right and you will feel less resentful about situations.

When people respond positively to what you say, you feel goodwill towards them, and they, equally, will value the fact that you are honest with them. For example, my butcher apologised profusely about the tough steak, deducted something from my next bill and now always makes sure that I'm well looked after. He values my custom and my honesty and I value his service and his attitude. It's an equal relationship.

Dealing assertively with any situation in everyday life, whether it's the butcher or the tax office, requires the same understanding of how we behave assertively that we learned about in earlier chapters. Assertiveness in any relationship is based on the same principles. Remind yourself of these guidelines before moving on to conquer the world. Over the page is an exercise for you to fill out.

1. *Know* how you feel and what you want.

2. *Say* how you feel and what you want.

3. *Listen* to what the other person feels and wants.

4. *Tell* him or her that you have heard his view.

5. *Repeat* what you want.

6. *Agree* a joint solution.

Think of a simple situation in your local community which you'd like to change. Write it down, say how you feel and what you would like to happen. For example: 'I can't stand queue jumpers. I feel angry when people push in. I'd like to say, "There's a queue here, would you wait for your turn".'

The situation _____

_____

_____

_____

What I feel _____

_____

_____

_____

_____

What I would like to happen _____

_____

_____

_____

_____

_____

Dealing with neighbours

As the words in the title song of the television series say, 'Neighbours, everybody needs good neighbours'. When relationships are good, everything is fine, but when problems arise it's important to tackle them early on: the children next door who play music at full blast when their parents are out; the young father, who is forever asking to borrow your lawn mower, or look after his children; the neighbour who refuses to share the cost of replacing the jointly owned drainpipe. Small incidents like these can so easily get blown up out of all proportion and quickly develop into major issues which last for years. Sometimes people can't even remember when they started.

Improving relationships

- If relationships with neighbours are good we value them. It makes sense to maintain them.

- If they're not too bad, but could be better, there's an incentive to sort things out and improve them.

- If relationships are problematic or fraught, it's always worth trying to improve things, while realising we may not always succeed.

Being a neighbour is a two-way process

What *they* do can affect you, and what *you* do can affect them. Step on to the other one's territory, for example, by putting a fence up, at your peril. If they cut down branches of your tree without mentioning it, you will probably react furiously. Behaving assertively means respecting their rights as well as sticking up for your own. If you behave this way then there's more chance they will behave the same way towards you. Being assertive in our dealings with neighbours means improving the way we communicate. It means being able to tell them clearly what we feel about things and them being able to do the same.

Tell them before you act Telling people what you are intending to do will prevent misunderstandings. For example, if you're going to put up a fence discuss it before embarking on the project. Asking how they feel about it, discussing whose ground the posts will go in and how high it will be, will allay any fears, and help to foster a relationship of honesty and openness which is what assertiveness is about. If they have objections they can say so, and you can talk it through, rather than having an enormous row after the fence is up.

Putting things right

When small things have gone wrong it's easy to put them right. You'll probably need to take the initiative, but the alternative is for things to get worse.

If things have already deteriorated, go slowly, and start practising improving your relationships with other neighbours before diving into a big or complicated problem.

Looking for solutions

Even if the problem is a long-standing one, there is no reason why you shouldn't consider raising the issue gently with your neighbour and seeing if you can find a solution. Ask if you can get together to talk about the situation. Making an approach in a spirit of compromise may get results. But be prepared for a rebuff and try not to act aggressively if that happens. Console yourself with the thought that at least you tried to resolve the problem.

Know what you want

It's no use going to complain about the loud music unless you know exactly what you want to happen. For example, you could say you're being disturbed by the very loud music late at night and you would like them to ask the children to keep the volume down. Listen to what they have to say. Being reasonable should prevent bad feeling and misunderstandings. Keep calm and if necessary re-state your position. Try to reach a mutual agreement.

Think of a situation you would like to resolve. Write it down, say how you feel and what you want to happen.

The situation _____

_____

_____

What I feel _____

_____

_____

What I want to happen _____

_____

_____

_____

Saying 'No' to neighbours

Sometimes it's very difficult to say 'No' to requests from neighbours, especially when they increase their demands almost without us noticing. It might start with borrowing a pint of milk, but suddenly they're wanting to borrow the lawn mower and then they're expecting us to look after their children when they're out.

Helping one another is one thing, but being taken advantage of is another. Learning to say 'No' firmly is essential. Remind yourself that you have rights, and that your neighbour is ignoring them and very selfishly expecting you to do what they want. You have the right to say 'No'.

Think back to a recent situation where you found yourself agreeing to a neighbour's request to do something you didn't want to do. Why did you agree? How did you feel afterwards?

Write down the situation and the request _____

_____

_____

How did you feel about it? _____

_____

_____

Why did you say 'Yes'? _____

_____

_____

What would you have liked to do? _____

_____

_____

Look at what you have written.

Now think about how you would tell the other person that

you don't want to do what he or she has asked. Say what you feel and say what you want to happen. In the case of a neighbour who always wants you to look after his children you would say, 'No, I can't. I feel that it's asking too much of me to have them every day, but I'll help if there's a real emergency'. Try thinking now about how you will say 'No' next time.

Your rights

When we are dealing with situations where we feel intimidated by pressure from individuals or overwhelmed by large organisations and authorities, it's good to remind ourselves of our rights. Remember also that individuals in positions of power or authority are only people who just happen to be in that position. We have equal rights with all other people. We have an equal right to have our voice heard too.

Thinking about your rights should make you feel good. Standing up for your rights and expressing your needs should make you feel more in control.

Here are some of your rights, add the others you feel are important:

- I have the right to be a member of the community.

- I have the right to be treated as an individual.

- I have the right to ask for my rights.

- I have the right to be treated as an equal.

- I have the right to be treated as a person not a number.

- I have the right to speak out.

- I have the right to be heard.

- I have the right to be _____

- I have the right to be _____

- I have the right to be _____

- I have the right to be _____

Dealing with the community

One reason for being assertive in your community is to make sure that, as a member of that community, your rights are looked after and you benefit from what you are entitled to. How you present yourself, and how others see you, will influence their attitude towards you and the way they treat you.

First impressions

People who don't know us very well make instant judgements based on our appearance. If you have a confident appearance and look as though you mean business, this will make a good first impression. Look back at Chapter One and body language (page 34).

Learn from other people Observe other people's behaviour.
- What does their body language tell you?
- Imagine if you were lost and needed help. Who would you choose to ask for directions?
- (a) Someone who looks nervous?
- (b) A red-faced and angry looking individual?
- (c) Someone who looks confident and at ease?

Observing aggressive, passive and assertive body language
Learn by watching other people's behaviour when they are trying to sort out a problem. One place where you will find plenty of examples is in a customer service department in a large store.

Watch the other people waiting to make complaints or return unwanted goods. Before they say anything you can tell some people are going to be aggressive. Their whole body gives off strong signals. Watch the assistant's reaction, it can result in a contest of wills and a less than helpful attitude. Of course, the opposite may happen. Watch as an embarrassed, apologetic (passive) customer approaches, and notice the assistant's behaviour. Sometimes he or she will appear disinterested or dismissive of the customer.

Keep an eye open for confident and assertive customers. They tend to sort out their problems quickly.

Acting assertively in public Developing a confident public appearance takes time, so don't be disheartened. Below is a simple exercise which will help you to get a feel of what 'being confident' can be like. You can practise without anyone else knowing.

Exercise: Decide to start acting in a very confident way with one very small piece of behaviour you do every day in the outside world. For example, closing your front door in a measured and confident way (refraining from your usual slam it and run); walking in an assured and confident way to the shops. You decide. Tell yourself, 'I feel confident doing this' and then allow yourself time to experience how it feels to act more confidently. There's no 'pass' or 'fail' attached to it. Once you begin to understand how it feels to act in a more positive way in public, you'll gain confidence to try out other behaviour in the same way. Perhaps you will try telling yourself that you feel more relaxed and assured as you wait at a customer service desk.

Write down what you are going to do _____

_____

_____

Try small things first and appreciate the experience of your body doing something in a different and more poised way.

Facing people with authority

Facing people with authority can sometimes seem rather frightening. Remembering to treat the individual as a person can help, but even so we all have different reactions to people in authority. Facing up to these reactions is a way of dealing with them and establishing more equal relationships.

Fear I remember as a child being absolutely awe-struck by people with authority – people who carried a big tag around their neck saying 'bank manager', 'doctor', 'policeman'. These tags often trigger off passive behaviour in adult life. Behaving assertively gives you confidence to overcome these irrational fears and face people with authority on an equal basis: asking the hospital consultant to explain what the diagnosis means could give you vital information about your options for treatment; your bank manager may be more reasonable about your overdraft if you communicate clearly and act more confidently with him.

Anger Sometimes the whole business of dealing with people who hide behind their authority becomes too much. I've seen people erupt into violent rages at unemployment offices when told that their file is missing and 'there's no one here who can look for it today'. Being assertive rather than aggressive in a situation like this may not change the end result, but it very clearly conveys the message that you mean business, and that you intend to persist until someone finds the file. It's a more reasonable way of behaving and it will leave you with a feeling of self-respect, and may just make your file reappear more quickly.

Frustration Dealing with large companies can make you want to scream or just give up. Behaving assertively and confronting organisations who try to 'pass the buck' can work, but you have to be persistent.

I recently had a problem with water finding its way into our house through a wall. The Water Board denied all responsibility and said it was rain coming in through the electricity cable (!). The Electricity Board said water was coming in via the gas pipe. The Gas Board said they could hear running water, but it wasn't a gas responsibility. After six months of silliness between all these authorities I took strong assertive action and insisted that the Water Board take up the pavement outside, otherwise I would take legal action. There was a hole the size of a walnut in the pipe. If the wall hadn't continued to drip water, I might have just given up in pure frustration. Many organisations work on this principle of hoping people will not be assertive or persistent. You can prove them wrong and make things better for yourself and for others.

Write down a specific situation where you have faced someone in a position of authority. How did you feel? How did you act? What would you have liked to do?

For example, after I separated from my husband I was looking for somewhere for the children and myself to live. I went to register with a local Cheshire estate agent who told me very authoritatively that this was a most unusual request, adding, 'Women don't act like this'. I would have liked to say, assertively, that my money was as good as any man's. Instead I felt angry and humiliated and crept away (passively). I fumed about it for days; this was the 1980s, not the Dark Ages!

The situation _____

_____

_____

I felt _____

_____

_____

I acted by _____

_____

_____

I would like to have _____

_____

_____

Dealing with official bodies

This is an opportunity to think about how being assertive could help you to deal with larger official organisations. Over the years we've had family experience of involvement with the Home Office over visas, appearances in Small Claims Courts, ongoing contacts with taxation departments and so on. Being assertive and clear in complex or difficult circumstances means people understand what we feel and what we want. In situations which are volatile, being calm and clear is essential.

Think of two or three important situations where acting assertively could be beneficial. These could be experiences you've had, or ones which might happen in the future where you can see the benefits of assertive behaviour. Use your imagination.

1. _____

2. _____

3. _____

Real people run them It sometimes seems that these large organisations are run by nameless and faceless automatons. Recognising that they are staffed by real people is the first step. Ask them for their names and write them down. The more assertive you are in your relationship with them, the better the outcome.

Be persistent Dealing with switchboards who put you on hold, or lose you, is the first problem, the next is when the manager is always 'out of the office'. Being assertive and persistent is the way forward.

Don't be intimidated Large institutions, anonymous company telephone voices, or officials quoting regulations can make you unsure of yourself. Don't let them intimidate you. Remember, *you* have the right to be heard. You are an equal member of the community. Say what you want and if necessary ask them to explain their official terminology clearly to you in plain English.

Know your limits

Knowing what you want and also knowing what you are entitled to, are two different things. Before you start trying to take on a large organisation make sure of your legal rights. It's no use asking assertively for things you're not entitled to – you will just end up very frustrated.

Dealing with the unexpected

By practising assertiveness in other areas of your life, you will gradually find that you are able to cope with most situations. All this will take time, but if something quite unexpected and unpleasant happens your assertive behaviour will automatically take over.

Obscene phone calls An assertive reaction to an obscene phone call may not solve the problem of the phone call, but it will help you to feel better about yourself. Once you have realised the nature of the call, deal with it as firmly as you can. Different people will do this in different ways, but as a guide, act quickly; you could say, for example, 'I think you have a wrong number', and put the phone down. Then report it to the telephone company. Remember, the person is trying to deny you your rights in a very unpleasant way. Don't let them.

Dealing with the aftermath of a burglary or a flood will be distressing, but in the chaos you will be able to stand back and assess what practical things you want to happen. For example, dealing assertively with an insurance company can produce a prompt response. Insurance companies tend to respond favourably to the assertive, honest and straightforward behaviour of policy holders who are in control of the situation and are clearly communicating their needs.

Your Personal Action Plan

Think about this chapter. What was the most important thing you learned? Write it down.

_____

_____

_____

_____

Start and stop

Think of a way of behaving in public which would help you to feel more assertive. For example, writing down all the things you want to say to the bank manager/doctor/tax man, before you see him. Decide to *start* using that behaviour. Then think of some behaviour which prevents you from feeling assertive. Decide to *stop* doing it. For example, walking into a crowded room with your head down, avoiding eye contact with people. Opposite is the Action Plan for you to fill in.

●

Being assertive sometimes means being persistent

●

Action Plan

I'm going to start _____

_____

_____

_____

_____

_____

_____

_____

_____

_____

I'm going to stop _____

_____

_____

_____

_____

_____

_____

_____

_____

_____

_____

Date _____

It goes on being useful

There always seem to be new situations cropping up where assertiveness can help you to get out of difficulties. Make it a rule always to think before you act, always to question why you are behaving in that particular way and to ask yourself if you are treating the other person as a person with rights too.

My current difficulty is dealing with the growing numbers of street beggars. I find it difficult to behave in an appropriate, assertive way, regardless of whether I give them money or not. But nobody said that being assertive is easy.

Assertiveness seems to grow with you, and whatever stage you are at in life you will find it useful. I have just become a grandmother and I am already developing a very rewarding (and assertive) relationship with my granddaughter.

Wherever you are starting from, I hope you have found this book interesting and helpful, and that it has encouraged you to feel confident in your ability to go on and tackle greater things.

●

Be assertive for a change

●

Scores for Exercises

Scoring for the Assertiveness Quizs on pages 10–11

					YOUR SCORE
(1)	a:3	b:2	c:1	d:4	[ ]
(2)	a:1	b:4	c:2	d:3	[ ]
(3)	a:4	b:3	c:2	d:1	[ ]
(4)	a:2	b:3	c:1	d:4	[ ]
(5)	a:3	b:2	c:4	d:1	[ ]
(6)	a:4	b:3	c:2	d:1	[ ]
(7)	a:2	b:3	c:4	d:1	[ ]
(8)	a:3	b:2	c:1	d:4	[ ]

Count up your score.   *Total* _____

A score of 8 indicates that your behaviour is aggressive.

Scores between 8 and 16 indicate that your behaviour is mainly aggressive but that in some situations you use manipulative behaviour.

Scores between 16 and 24 indicate a more passive type of behaviour.

Scores between 24 and 30 indicate that you already behave assertively in many situations and probably use passive behaviour from time to time.

Scores over 30 indicate that you are a very assertive person.

Key to the Work Situation questionnaire on page 91

In most cases A would be Aggressive.
In most cases B could be Passive.
In most cases C would be both Passive and Aggressive.
In most cases D would be Assertive.
In most cases E would be Assertive.
In most cases F would be Assertive.

What do you think you would do?

Assertiveness Courses

If you want to learn more about assertiveness training you may find it useful to go on a course where you will work with a small group of people. You will find information about courses through your local public library or information centre. They will have contact names and addresses.

Further Reading

If you want to read more about assertiveness you may find the following books helpful.

Back, Ken and Kate, *Assertiveness at Work*, McGraw Hill, 1982.

Dickson, Anne, *A Woman in your own Right*, Quartet, 1982.

Hare, Beverley, *Be Assertive*, Optima, 1988.

Holland, Stephanie and Ward, Clare, *Assertiveness: A Practical Approach*, Winslow Press, 1991.

Lindenfield, Gael, *Assert Yourself*, Thorsons, 1986.

Lindenfield, Gael, *Super Confidence*, Thorsons, 1989.

Miles, Rosalind, *Danger: Men at Work*, Macdonald Futura, 1983.

Pease, Alan, *Body Language*, Sheldon Press, 1981.

Smith, Manuel J., *When I say No I feel Guilty*, Bantam, 1981.

Taylor, Bryce, *Assertiveness and the Management of Conflict*, Oasis, 1989.

Townend, Anni, *Assertion Training*, FPA Education Unit, 1985.

Willis, Liz and Daisley, Jenny, *Springboard. Women's Development Workbook*, Hawthorn Press, 1990.